1502340070
AF836656

The Direction of Trade Policy

The Direction of Trade Policy

Papers in Honor of Isaiah Frank

Edited by Charles S. Pearson and James Riedel

Basil Blackwell

Copyright © Basil Blackwell 1990

First published 1990

Basil Blackwell, Inc.
3 Cambridge Center
Cambridge, Massachusetts 02142, USA

Basil Blackwell Ltd
108 Cowley Road, Oxford OX4 1JF, UK

All rights reserved. Except for the quotation of short passages for the purposes of criticism and review, no part of this publication may be reproduced, stored in a retrieval system, or transmitted, in any form or by any means, electronic, mechanical, photocopying, recording or otherwise, without the prior permission of the publisher.

Except in the United States of America, this book is sold subject to the condition that it shall not, by way of trade or otherwise, be lent, re-sold, hired out, or otherwise circulated without the publisher's prior consent in any form of binding or cover other than that in which it is published and without a similar condition including this condition being imposed on the subsequent purchaser.

Library of Congress Cataloging in Publication Data
The Direction of Trade Policy/edited by Charles Pearson and James Riedel.
p. cm.
Includes bibliographical references.
ISBN 1-55786-080-7
1. Developing countries--Commercial policy. 2. United States--Commercial policy. 3. Free trade. 4. Protectionism. I. Pearson, Charles S. II. Riedel, James.
HF1413.D55 1990
382′.3′0973--dc20

89-18656
CIP

British Library Cataloguing in Publication Data
A CIP catalogue record for this book is available from the British Library.

HF 1413 DIR

WITHDRAWN

24 JAN 2022

Typeset in 10 on 12 pt Ehrhardt
by Best-set Typesetter Ltd.
Printed in Great Britain by T. J. Press, Padstow, Cornwall

UNIVERSITY OF BRISTOL

UNIVERSITY
OF BRISTOL
LIBRARY

Contents

Contributors

Bela Balassa Professor of Economics, The Johns Hopkins University, and Consultant to the World Bank

Robert E. Baldwin Professor of Economics, University of Wisconsin – Madison

W. Max Corden Professor of International Economics, School of Advanced International Studies, The Johns Hopkins University

Enzo Grilli Chief Economist, Economic Advisory Staff, the World Bank, and Professorial Lecturer, School of Advanced International Studies, The Johns Hopkins University

Anne O. Krueger Arts and Sciences Professor of Economics, Duke University

Charles S. Pearson Director and Professor of International Economics, School of Advanced International Studies, The Johns Hopkins University

James Riedel Professor of International Economics, School of Advanced International Studies, The Johns Hopkins University

Wendy E. Takacs Associate Professor of Economics, University of Maryland, Baltimore County, and Professorial Lecturer, School of Advanced International Studies, The Johns Hopkins University

Preface

All of the papers contained in this volume except those of the editors were presented at a symposium on "The Direction of Trade Policy", held at the Paul H. Nitze School of Advanced International Studies (SAIS) of The Johns Hopkins University in November, 1988. The topic itself is of sufficient interest to warrant a symposium, but we had a larger purpose, to honor our colleague and friend Isaiah Frank, William L. Clayton Professor of International Economics and for 25 years Director of the Program in International Economics at SAIS. The topic of the symposium is one to which Isaiah has made many important contributions, and the authors of the papers in this volume are all people with whom Isaiah has worked closely over the years, in some cases as a teacher, in others as a university colleague or an associate at the World Bank. Everyone responded to our invitation to contribute a paper or serve as a discussant at the symposium with enormous enthusiasm because of the opportunity it offered to honor Isaiah Frank. Such is the admiration and esteem in which Isaiah is held by his colleagues and friends.

In putting this volume together many debts were incurred and many thanks are due. We first would like to thank the authors for their unfailing cooperation. We are indebted to Simon Serfaty, Executive Director of The Johns Hopkins University Foreign Policy Institute and to George Packard, Dean of the School of Advanced International Studies, for their support and encouragement. Last, but far from least, we owe a debt of gratitude to Mary Hiatt, until recently the coordinator of the International Economics Program at the School of Advanced International Studies, who attended to most of the organizational responsibilities of running the symposium and editing this volume.

Introduction

This book is about the direction of trade policy. However, trade policy does not move in a single direction; different countries chart very different courses for trade policy. Some are clearly liberalizing, others are drifting toward protectionism, and some are simultaneously liberalizing trade in some sectors while raising barriers in other sectors of their economies. Nor does trade policy in a given country move in one direction over time, but rather appears to travel in circles – sometimes in the direction of liberalization, sometimes pushed by the strong winds of protectionism. Not surprisingly, we find that most of the issues and instruments of trade policy that are important today were present in the nineteenth century, or even earlier.

On the surface, therefore, trade policy does not appear to move in a clearly discernable direction, but rather more closely resembles the Brownian movement of dust particles, swept along by intellectual and political cross-currents. Nevertheless, beneath the surface it is possible to identify two broad currents in trade policy in the second half of the postwar era. These currents are moving in opposite directions. Starting sometime in the late 1960s, progress toward liberal trade, which had characterized the early postwar years, lost momentum in the industrial countries. By the 1980s there was a measurable increase in protectionism, although in some areas, most notably through the Uruguay Round, liberalization efforts continue. The change is broader than an increase in import barriers alone. Quantitative and discriminatory restraints have (again) become popular; unilateralism and regionalism have staged a comeback; and the GATT system is in some disarray.

In the meantime, in developing countries the great experiment with import substitution ran its course, although important vestiges remain. Partly through the remarkable demonstration effect by the East Asian countries, partly through equally remarkable failures of excessive import substitution, and partly (and ironically) through pressures from the industrial countries, many developing countries are moving toward more liberal trade regimes.

These, then, are the two directions or currents in trade policy which the authors of this book analyze. Each current has unique features.

For the industrial countries, and the United States in particular, three features stand out. The first is the (re)enshrinement of fair trade, not free trade, as the cornerstone of policy. Second, macroeconomic imbalances have become pronounced and the cause-and-effect relationship between trade policy and external imbalances are joined by the policy maker, and require analytical attention. Finally, a combination of factors – rapid shifts in comparative advantage, the urge to assist development, and the debt problem – all combine to make the trade policy of industrial countries toward developing countries worthy of separate analysis.

At the broadest level, the developing countries are moving toward more liberal trade, although progress is fitful. Lingering concern about expansion of exports that might depress the terms of trade – the fallacy of composition argument – and legitimate concern about rising protectionism in the industrial countries, are partly responsible for guarded adoption of export oriented trade regimes. The compelling need to service external debt limits the removal of import restrictions. Thus the timing, scale, and durability of trade liberalization shows great disparities among developing countries. Nevertheless, the growing recognition by developing countries that the liberal principles of the GATT system can serve their interests is an important development.

This book is organized around these two principal currents in trade policy. Part I considers the trade policy of industrial countries, primarily the United States. Robert Baldwin and Charles Pearson set the stage by offering complimentary interpretations of the changes in US trade policy. Baldwin's central premise is that the evolution of US commercial policy reflects its declining hegemonic role in the global economy. The relative decline of the United States from its pre-eminent position at the end of World War II was exacerbated in the early 1980s by macroeconomic policies and the resulting strong dollar. These two shifts led to the priority of perceived domestic commercial interests over foreign policy goals, and an unwillingness to prop up a liberal trade system and provide that system to the world as a "public good," an ideal incidentally that has mercantilist connotations. In any event, the massive US trade deficits of the 1980s were the cue that "fair traders" were waiting for, and domestic politics has helped shape both increases in protection and the new aggressive reciprocity.

Pearson asks a deceptively simple question. Why was it that the Reagan administration, with a strong ideological commitment to *laissez faire* and to free market economics, not only failed to free up international trade, but allowed or encouraged a considerable retreat from the principles of liberal trade? Part of his answer lies in showing that the "modern" trade issues dealt with in the 1980s have roots deep in US commercial history, and that the commitment to liberal trade was a relatively brief affair. Part of his answer is that there was no spokesman at the highest level of government who saw free trade as the logical corollary to Reaganomics – in short, politics dominated principle.

United States trade policy toward developing countries exhibits more than the usual ambivalence. A generalized system of preferences is offered, preferential trade arrangements are extended, and the virtues of liberalizing trade regimes are preached. At the same time, new competition in manufactures presents an uncomfortable challenge, and the United States complains of the "burden" of absorbing disproportionate imports from the Third World. Bela Balassa assembles and interprets the evidence. Within the limits of data and method, he finds that Europe and Japan are more restrictive than the United States in both manufactures and agricultural products. In the tricky area of countervailing duties, he finds that there was a surge of actions by the United States directed toward developing countries in the first half of the 1980s, but that they have slowed in recent years.

Trade policy is made within a macroeconomic context and conceivably can have measurable macroeconomic consequences. Max Corden takes as his point of departure the present structural imbalances between the major surplus and deficit industrial countries. With precise logic he traces the effect of trade policy on current account balances. The general answer is given by the national income accounting framework he employs – everything depends on how one chooses to model the effects of import restraints on absorption and in particular on domestic savings and investment. It is, however, his discussion of the effect of macro-imbalance on trade policy, and especially his elaboration of the concept of conservative resistance, that ties his analysis to the political economy of trade policy.

For Corden, conservative resistance blends the idea of a social welfare function that protects against substantial income losses to specific groups, with the idea that pressure groups are willing to spend more resources to protect against income loss than to ensure income gain.

During the same period that the industrial countries have been edging away from the principles of liberal trade – though certainly not the full practice – some developing countries found that an export oriented strategy paid handsome dividends. And despite the unproductive diversion of obtaining formalized "special and differential" treatment in the Kennedy Round, a few are beginning to see how a revitalized GATT might protect them against some of the harsher protectionist measures they now face. This is the central theme of Part II.

James Riedel deals first and foremost with the intellectual battles in which the "outward looking" strategists took victory from the "inward looking" strategists. He makes two important points. First, this is not a victory for free trade. At best, it is a victory for a trade-neutral strategy wherein the equality of the average effective exchange rates for exports and imports can conceal substantial import substitution and net export subsidies in individual sectors. Second, a positive role for import substitution in the early phase of industrialization still has not been rejected. His conclusion, that the outward–inward policy debate was won through superior performance, and not by theoretical argument, is telling.

Anne Krueger stays mainly with the empirical evidence, and reminds us of the diversity of policy reactions in developing countries to the harsh trade environment of the 1980s. In some debtor countries, the severity of the crisis has compelled significant adjustment, including trade liberalization. She cites Bolivia, Mexico, and Uruguay. In others, however, external debt service requirements have reversed earlier trade liberalization, often through tighter quantitative restrictions, although realignment and real devaluations of exchange rates have frequently been used to improve the trade balance.

Apart from the immediate problems of debt, developing countries have hesitated to fully commit themselves to an export-based strategy because of fears about the terms of trade and protectionism. The first suggest that, although the international price elasticity of demand for manufactures from an individual country may be high, the success of the original newly industrializing countries (NICs) cannot be widely replicated without depressing the terms of trade, an idea that neglects strong evidence that countries occupy and move along different rungs of a product sophistication ladder. Enzo Grilli touches on the terms of trade argument, but is principally concerned with protectionism that limits access to the industrial country market, and with how the developing countries have responded. He demonstrates that geographic market diversification, upgrading, product diversification, cost control, and skillful penetration of porous trade barriers in industrial countries, have all contributed to success in exporting manufactures, despite the adverse international economic climate.

One feature of the "new trade policy" is extensive use of quantitative and often discriminatory restraints imposed under the Multifiber Arrangement or under the guise of orderly marketing agreements and voluntary export agreements. Quantitative restraints are also still widely used by developing countries. If there is to be a return to GATT principles, practical measure will have to be found to dismantle this structure of protection. Assuming that countries may wish to move toward less distortive measures, or indeed toward free trade, Wendy Takacs sets up the question: What transitional measures are best suited on grounds of efficiency, equity, and pragmatism to move toward a tariffs-only regime? In her carefully reasoned assessment of alternatives, no single scheme emerges as the clear choice, although the use of a tariff-rate quota, which in normal circumstances has little to recommend it, does show redemptive value as a transitional device.

Charles S. Pearson
and James Riedel

Part I

The US and Global Perspectives

1

US Trade Policy, 1945–1988: From Foreign Policy to Domestic Policy

Robert E. Baldwin

1 Introduction

There have been major changes in US trade policies in the 1970s and 1980s. From the end of World War II through the Kennedy Round of trade negotiations in the 1960s, the United States was the world's leader in promoting multilateral trade liberalization, mainly as a means of implementing its foreign policy goals. American tariffs on dutiable imports dropped from an average of about 35 percent in the early 1940s to only about 7 percent by the end of the 1960s. While not opposing regional trade agreements for some countries, the United States strongly favored a nondiscriminatory approach to liberalization during this period.

Since the 1970s, the United States has stressed "fair" trade more than free trade. In the current Uruguay Round, for example, only in agriculture and trade in services are American negotiators pressing for liberalization. Most of their other efforts are devoted to tightening and more strictly enforcing existing GATT rules on such activities as government subsidization and dumping, and to formulating new GATT rules aimed at reducing counterfeiting and at increasing the protection of intellectual property rights. Not only is trade liberalization no longer a major goal of US international economic policy, but the United States is now a leading user of nontariff barriers (NTBs) as a means of curtailing imports. Among industrialized countries, only France, Australia, Finland, and Switzerland had a larger proportion of products subject to NTBs in 1983 than the United States, according to a World Bank study by Nogues, Olechowski, and Winters (1985). (If fuels are eliminated from the product coverage, the United States ranks slightly below the average percentage of product covered for all industrial countries.) Furthermore, most of the NTBs introduced have been discriminatory in the sense of being applicable only to selected countries.

There has also been a much greater willingness in recent years to participate in exclusive regional liberalization agreements. The United States has, for example, granted special trade and investment privileges to countries in the Caribbean Basin, entered into a free trade arrangement with Israel, negotiated a sweeping free trade agreement with Canada, and initiated bilateral liberalization with Mexico. Furthermore, the view is now widely held in the United States that the multilateral liberalizing negotiations of the 1940s, 1950s, and 1960s did not open the markets of foreign countries to the extent that they opened American markets and that vigorous bilateral efforts to open foreign markets are, therefore, now necessary. In the Omnibus Trade and Competitiveness Act of 1988 the US Trade Representative is directed to take retaliatory actions against countries that deny fair and equitable market opportunities to US producers.

This chapter analyzes the various economic and political factors that have led to these shifts in US trade policies and considers how well they will serve US interests in the 1990s and beyond. Section 2 discusses the nature of the trade policies pursued by the United States as it became the dominant world economic power after World War II, while section 3 analyzes how basic structural changes in the world economy brought about a decline in US hegemony and the concomitant rise to international economic prominence of the European Community and Japan, and the emergence of a group of newly industrializing developing countries. In section 4, it is argued that these structural changes, coupled with US macroeconomic policies leading to a sharp appreciation of the dollar in the first part of the 1980s and to a massive US trade deficit, have led to significant trade-policy shifts that emphasize the priority of domestic interests over foreign policy goals. Section 5 appraises the effectiveness of these new trade policies in meeting the international economic challenges the United States is likely to face in the 1990s and the early part of the next century, while section 6 summarizes the conclusions.

2 The emergence of US hegemony

The expansion of productive facilities in the United States during World War II, coupled with the widespread destruction of industrial capacity in Germany and Japan, gave American producers an enormous advantage in meeting the worldwide pent-up demand of the late 1940s and the 1950s. The US share of industrial country exports rose from 25.6 percent in 1938 to 35.2 percent in 1952 (Baldwin, 1958). In contrast, the combined share of Germany and Japan fell from 24.0 percent to 11.4 percent between these years. Thus the United States became the dominant economic trading power in the period immediately following World War II.

Due to the failure of the United Kingdom to return to anything like its prewar position as a world economic power, and the unwillingness of either China or the USSR to participate in a market-oriented international economy, the United States also became the dominant political power in the nonsocialist world economy. But perhaps the most important factor leading to US hegemony was the effort by the Soviet Union to expand its political influence into Western Europe and elsewhere. American officials believed they had little choice from a national viewpoint but to assume an active political, economic and military leadership role in the world to counter this expansionist policy, an action that most noncommunist countries welcomed.

Static trade theory suggests that a hegemonic power will take advantage of its monopolistic position by imposing trade restrictions to raise domestic welfare through an improvement in its terms of trade. However, like the United Kingdom when it was a hegemonic nation in the 19th century, the United States reacted by promoting trade liberalization rather than trade restrictionism. A restrictionist reaction might have been possible for a highly controlled, planned economy that could redistribute income fairly easily and did not need to rely on the traded-goods sector as a major source of employment generation or growth. But the growth goals of free-market firms, together with the nature of the political decision-making process, rule out such a response in modern nonsocialist industrial democracies.

Industrial organization theory emphasizes that firms in oligopolistically organized industries take a long-term view of profitability and strive to increase their market share. By doing so, they try to prevent both new competitors from entering the market and possibly causing losses to existing firms, and old competitors from increasing their shares to the point where others might suffer progressive and irreversible market losses. American firms, organized in this manner, seized the postwar competitive opportunities associated with American dominance to expand overseas market shares both through increased exports and direct foreign investment. The desire of US political leaders to strengthen noncommunist nations by opening up American markets and providing foreign aid complemented the goals of US business, and most business leaders actively supported the government's foreign policy aims. Even in more competitively organized, less technologically sophisticated sectors such as textiles and miscellaneous manufactures, most producers favored an outward-oriented hegemonic policy at this time, since they too were able to export abroad and were not faced with significant import competition.

The United States behaved in a hegemonic manner on many occasions in the 1950s and early 1960s. As Keohane (1984, chapter 8) emphasizes, the United States, in doing this, did not coerce other states into accepting policies of little benefit to them. Instead, the United States usually proposed joint policy efforts in areas of mutual economic interest and provided strong incentives for hegemonic cooperation. In the trade field, for example, US officials regularly pressed for trade-liberalizing multilateral negotiations, and six such negotiations were initiated between 1947 and 1962. The United States traded short-term concessions for the prospect of long-term gains, since the concessions by most other countries were not very meaningful in trade terms due to the exchange controls they maintained until the late 1950s. The economic goal was to increase US market shares in Europe and Japan significantly as these countries eased and finally eliminated their controls over imports.

The hegemonic actions of the United States aimed at maintaining a liberal international economic framework and strengthening the noncommunist countries of the world as a means of turning back the expansion of the Soviet Union succeeded very well. By 1960 the export market shares of France, Germany, Italy, and Japan had either exceeded or come close to their prewar levels. Among the industrial countries only the United Kingdom had failed to regain its prewar position by this time. The restoration of peacetime productive capabilities in these countries meant, however, that the exceptionally high market shares of the United States in the early postwar years declined correspondingly. The 35.2 percent US export share of 1952 had dropped to 29.9 percent by 1960, a figure that was, however, still higher than the US share of 25.6 percent in 1938 (Baldwin, 1962).

For manufactured products alone, the picture is much the same. The US world export share decreased sharply from 29.4 percent in 1953 to 18.7 percent in 1959, while the shares of Western Europe and Japan rose from 49.0 to 53.7 percent and from 2.8 to 4.9 percent respectively (Branson, 1980). The export market share of Western Europe remained unchanged in the 1960s, but the Japanese share continued to rise and reached 10.0 percent in 1971, a year in which the US share of world exports of manufactures fell to 13.4 percent.

3 The decline in US economic dominance

Not only had the prewar export position of the United States been restored by the late 1960s, but the absence of significant import pressures in major industries with political clout had come to an end. Stiff competition from the Japanese in the cotton textiles industry was evident by the late 1950s, and the United States initiated the formation of a trade-restricting international cotton textile agreement in 1962. A broad group of other industries began to face significant import competition in the late 1960s as the dollar became progressively overvalued. The products affected included footwear, radios and television sets, tires and inner tubes, semiconductors, hand tools, earthenware table and kitchen articles, jewelry, and some steel items.

Changes in trade patterns in the 1970s and early 1980s were much influenced by the price-increasing actions of the Organization of Petroleum Exporting Countries (OPEC). This group's share of world exports rose from 5.4 percent in 1970 to 14.6 percent in 1980 (*Economic Report of the President*, 1985). By 1985, however, OPEC's share had fallen to 7.1 percent, as the power of the cartel declined (*Economic Report of the President*, 1986). From 1970 to 1980 the US world export share fell from 13.8 to 10.8 percent, while that of the European Community dropped from 36.2 to 32.6 percent. Japan only managed to increase its share from 6.1 to 6.3 percent.

In the manufacturing sector alone, the 1970s were a period of market share stability for the United States, as US competitiveness benefited from the dollar depreciation in the early part of the decade. The US share of manufacturing exports from industrial countries was 18.3 percent in both 1972 and 1980 (US Department of Commerce, 1985). Japan's share rose from 10.2 percent in 1972 to 11.9 percent in 1980, while the Community's share decreased from 60.8 to 59.6 percent between these years.

Another important feature of the trade-pattern shifts in industrial countries during the 1970s and 1980s was the severe import competition faced not only by labor-intensive sectors like textiles, apparel, and footwear, but also by large-scale, oligopolistically-organized industries such as steel, automobiles, and shipbuilding. Machine tools and consumer electronic goods also came under increasing import pressure.

The decline in the dominance of the United States in trade-policy matters became apparent in the Tokyo Round of multilateral trade negotiations as well as when the United States proposed a new negotiating round in 1982. As it had in the Kennedy Round, the United States proposed an across-the-board linear tariff-cutting rule at the outset of the Tokyo Round, whereas the European Community again proposed a formula that cut high tariff rates by a greater percentage than low duties. This time the United States was not able to impose its negotiating wishes. The other participants treated the United States and the Community as two major trading blocs whose broad negotiating objectives must both be satisfied. The compromise duty-cutting rule adopted met the US desire for a deep average cut and at the same time produced the degree of tariff harmonization sought by the European Community.

At the 1982 GATT ministerial meeting the United States again called for new multilateral negotiations aimed at reducing export subsidies in agriculture and extending GATT rules to trade in services. The Community and the developing countries both rejected the US proposals. Although these proposals were eventually placed on the agenda for the Uruguay

Round beginning in 1986, it has become clear that the timing and nature of multilateral trade negotiations will no longer be determined largely by the United States.

4 The US trade-policy response

Except for the two politically powerful industries (oil and textiles), import-injured industries, up until the latter part of the 1960s, were forced to follow the administrative route for providing import relief under the escape clause provisions of the GATT. Moreover, many of the affirmative industry determinations by the International Trade Commission under this procedure were rejected by the president on foreign policy grounds, specifically, the need for the hegemonic power to maintain an open trade policy. Industry subsidies provided by foreign governments, though subject to US countervailing duty laws, were also largely ignored by the executive branch for the same reason.

The official position of the United States began to change under the strong import pressures of the late 1960s. As their constituents described the competitive problems they were facing, members of Congress became less willing to accept the standard argument that a liberal US trade policy was essential to strengthen the free world against communism. The change in members' views is indicated by the rejection by Congress of President Lyndon Johnson's 1968 request for new trade authority and by its near approval in 1970 of protectionist legislation. The growing unwillingness of the allies of the United States to accept her unquestioned leadership in international political, military, and economic affairs also caused officials in the executive branch to question the traditional American position on trade policy.

A view that gradually began to gain the support of private interests concerned with trade matters was that much of the increased competitive pressure on the United States was due to unfair foreign policies such as government subsidization, dumping by private and public firms, preferential government purchasing procedures, and discriminatory foreign administrative rules and practices relating to importation. This argument had appeal for several reasons. No new legislation was required to provide import relief; a stricter enforcement of long-existing domestic legislation seemed to be all that was necessary. By placing the blame for their decline in competitiveness on unfair foreign actions, US managers and workers could also avoid the implication that increased import pressures might be due to a decline in their efficiency relative to certain other countries. Finally, US government officials could maintain they were still supporting the rules of the liberal international regime that the United States had played such a major role in designing.

Emphasis on the greater need for fair trade is evident in the 1974 legislation authorizing US participation in the Tokyo Round of multilateral negotiations. In reshaping the proposal of the president, Congress stressed that the president should seek "to harmonize, reduce, or eliminate" nontariff trade barriers and tighten GATT rules with respect to fair trading practices. Officials in the executive branch supported these directives not only on their merits but because they deflected attention from more patently protectionist policies.

It was, however, the emergence of a massive US trade deficit, beginning in the late 1970s and becoming especially severe after 1982, that gave the greatest impetus to the acceptance of the view that a major cause of US competitive problems was unfair trade actions by foreign governments. This deficit had its roots in the significant fall in aggregate savings brought about by the increase in federal government expenditures relative to tax collections. Since private savings did not increase to offset this decline in government savings, the effect of the increase in federal government expenditures had to be a crowding out of either domestic investment or net foreign investment. The rise of interest rates as the government bid for funds and the Federal Reserve pursued a tight monetary policy to halt the double-digit inflation that had emerged not only tended to discourage private investment but attracted a large inflow of foreign funds and a return of US funds previously invested abroad. Consequently, as the international demand for dollars increased and the trade balance turned sharply negative, the value of the dollar rose significantly compared to its value in the late 1970s. Other factors that contributed to the deficit were the slow rate of growth in many other countries, tax changes in the United States that made US investments more attractive, and the removal by the Japanese government of certain controls over foreign investment.

The sharp appreciation of the dollar not only exacerbated the profitability difficulties of such "problem" import-competing industries as textiles and apparel, footwear, steel, and automobiles, but brought significant international competitive pressures to most traditionally vigorous export-oriented and import-competing industries. The widespread nature of this competitive problem caused the trade deficit to be a matter of serious concern to almost all members of Congress and most parts of the executive branch.

Both Congress and the administration faced difficult political problems in trying to correct the conditions causing both the budget and trade deficits. President Reagan had pledged not to raise taxes and was also committed to large defense expenditures. Cutting social spending was the Administration's proposal for solving the problem. Members of Congress, especially the

Democrats, rejected this approach both on ideological grounds and for fear of disapproval by their constituents. Voting for an increase in taxes, especially when the president was likely to veto such a bill, also was not a politically feasible alternative for Congress. Instead, more and more members of Congress began to adopt the view that the unwillingness of foreign governments to open their domestic markets to the extent that the United States had already done was a major cause of the US trade problem. Blaming foreigners did not involve the risk of voter disapproval that raising taxes or cutting social or defense expenditures did. The fact that the administration had not made widespread use of this argument also made it attractive as a way of shifting blame for the trade deficit problem from Congress to the administration.

Implying that the main cause of the large US trade deficit with most countries is the failure of these countries to open their domestic markets sufficiently has proved to be very popular with voters, and most members of Congress seem to have adopted this view. This was evident from the nature of the trade bills that passed both branches of Congress in 1987. The House bill required the US Trade Representative (USTR) to determine whether "excessive surplus countries" maintain a pattern of unfair trade practices and then to negotiate with these countries to eliminate the practices. If the negotiations failed, USTR was required to take action to reduce the surpluses of these countries by 10 percent a year. The president could waive this retaliation but Congress could override the waiver by a two-thirds vote. The Senate bill did not explicitly link trade surpluses and unfair trade practices but required USTR to determine which countries maintain a consistent pattern of unfair trade practices against US exports and then to negotiate agreements eliminating these practices. Retaliation would follow if these negotiations failed.

Because of objections by the executive branch, these various provisions explicitly linking unfair foreign trade practices and the US deficit were omitted from the legislation finally passed, namely, the Omnibus Trade and Competitiveness Act of 1988. Nevertheless, eliminating unfair trade practices by foreign governments is still the central theme of this measure.

The widespread support in Congress for a tougher trade policy forced the Reagan administration to adopt a much more aggressive approach than it followed in its early years. The US government has, for example, retaliated against the Japanese for alleged dumping of computer chips in the United States and in third-country markets, drawn up a list of retaliatory items against Brazil in an effort to open this market to US computers and computer software, and threatened retaliation against the South Koreans unless they further opened their markets for cigarettes and beef. A greater emphasis on fair trade is also evident from the marked increase in the number of antidumping and countervailing duty cases. Between 1980 and 1985 the number of cases initiated rose from 30 to 104.

The unfair trade argument has also been used in support of most other trade-restricting or trade-promoting actions taken by the United States in recent years. The textile and apparel sectors have been described by government officials as "beleaguered" by disruptive import surges, thus justifying more restrictive import controls. Similarly, when temporary orderly marketing agreements (OMAs) were negotiated in the 1970s with selected East and Southeast Asian countries, the implication conveyed was that the agreements were responses to unfair export activities by these nations. Even the Japanese voluntary export restraint on automobiles was sometimes justified by American industry and government officials on the grounds that the industry's competitive problem was in part due to the unfair targeting practices of the Japanese government. On the export-promoting side, it is routinely claimed that subsidized export credits through the Export-Import Bank and special tax privileges to exporters are necessary to counter unfair foreign practices in these areas. In short, fair trade arguments using such phrases as the need for "a level playing field" or "to make foreign markets as open as US markets" have become the basic justification for the greater use of trade-distorting measures by the United States.

5 An evaluation of recent US trade policies

The immediate purpose of the vigorous US efforts to open foreign markets has been to reduce the US bilateral deficits with most countries. While these efforts may succeed in cutting the deficits somewhat, it is doubtful that trade barriers by other countries have been a cause of the US trade deficit. As late as 1981, the United States had a current account surplus of $7 billion and a merchandise account deficit of only $27 billion (in contrast to a $145 billion merchandise deficit in 1987). While in 1981 there were US trade deficits with Japan and Canada of $16 billion and $2 billion respectively, there were US trade surpluses with Western Europe and the non-OPEC developing countries of $7 billion and $300 million respectively. The record shows that Japan and the non-OPEC developing countries have generally been lowering their trade barriers against US exports since the early 1980s. Consequently, it is hard to argue that the trade balance shifts resulting in 1987 US deficits of $56 billion and $12 billion with Japan and Canada respectively, and of $26 billion and $52 billion with Western Europe and the non-OPEC developing countries, are due to new trade barriers in these countries.

Of course, if these markets had been more open, the US macroeconomic policies that are the major cause of the US trade problem might not have produced as large a deficit as in fact emerged. But there is disagreement among trade specialists as to whether import ratios are artificially low in countries such as Japan or the newly industrializing countries (NICs) in Asia because of unusually high nontariff trade barriers. Saxonhouse (1983, 1985), Bergsten and Cline (1985), and Noland (1987), for example, all find Japan's trading pattern to be explained adequately by the same basic real factors that account for the trade of other countries, and they reject the hypothesis that Japanese trade barriers are a major explanatory factor. In contrast, Balassa (1986) and Lawrence (1987) find that unusual trade barriers in Japan do play a role in accounting for the Japanese trade surplus. Lawrence, for example, estimates that the removal of unusual trade barriers would lower Japan's total trade surplus in manufactured goods by about $9 billion. This would mean a reduction of about $4 billion, or only 7 percent, in the $56 billion US deficit with Japan. A recent multicountry study by Leamer (1988) of the role of hidden trade barriers in accounting for trade patterns concludes that "unusual aspects of patterns of net exports occur most frequently from the export side and are related to historical factors or to special resources, and not to trade barriers."

If one concludes that US bilateral efforts to reduce nontariff trade barriers in other countries, even if successful, will not reduce the US trade deficit appreciably, it still could be argued that these efforts are worthwhile because they tend to raise world real income and, most probably, real income in the countries reducing the barriers. Possible adverse political effects might result, however, from the resentment generated by so-called Japan- and Korea-bashing by US officials. Americans might find that these countries will not support the foreign policy goals of the United States as vigorously as they would wish because of this weakening of good will toward the United States.

More tangible economic losses are possible in the long run. Japan and most developing countries have been urged to turn their demand-creating activities inward rather than rely so much on exports as a source of growth. If this advice is followed, it will mean that import-substituting activities will be stressed more strongly by the governments of these countries and, therefore, that US exporters of goods and services will face increased competition from domestic producers in these countries. Current US trade policies also encourage the strengthening of such regional groups as ASEAN and the formation of new regional arrangements. Since these groups provide special trade preferences for their members, countries like the United States lose export markets through the trade diversion that occurs.

The importance of favorable export markets for US products has increased in recent years because of the growing net debtor position of the

United States. This net debtor position is estimated to have grown by $150 billion in 1987 to a net position of $400 billion. While the income required to service this debt is less than one-half of one percent of the US GNP, at a 5 percent real rate of return, by the end of the century, servicing claims will consume 2 percent of the GNP at this rate (*Economic Report of the President*, 1988.) The ability of the United States to export becomes increasingly important as these servicing charges rise. Yet the current US policy of, in effect, favoring bilateral trade balance as the desirable norm may be turned against the United States when US export surpluses become important for servicing the net foreign debt.

The desirability of negotiating additional free trade agreements with other trading partners as a means of furthering US long-term international economic interests also seems questionable. The most successful free trade agreements or customs unions involve geographically close countries with special political relationships. Trade creation tends to be greater than trade diversion, thereby minimizing the resentment of third countries, and the economic adjustments involved in such arrangements become more acceptable because of the close political ties.

The US agreements with Canada and Israel satisfy these conditions, but there does not seem to be any additional scope for successful free trade agreements except, perhaps, for more extensive agreements with Mexico and the Caribbean nations. In the case of Japan, for example, the difficulty faced by US producers in penetrating Japanese domestic markets seems to be due to factors that will not be affected by such agreements. Agreements with various distant developing countries carry the risk that, to achieve an acceptable degree of reciprocity for the United States, these countries will restrict imports from third countries which, in turn, will divert exports to the United States and may be forced to reduce their US imports. This can not only exacerbate US problems of economic adjustment, but can slow growth and can increase political animosity against the United States in important parts of the developing world. A more appropriate strategy would seem to be the GATT multilateral approach, which would be aimed at creating the kind of general trade liberalization best suited to US export capabilities and import needs, coupled with a judicious use of bilateral negotiations to open markets in particular countries that are reluctant to accept the liberalization responsibilities of the GATT.

As noted in section 1, another feature of recent US trade policy is its discriminatory form. Antidumping and countervailing duties are, of course, levied on a country-specific basic, but in responding to import injury not based on unfair trade practices, the United States has also been adopting country-selective protection rather than protecting on a most-favored-nation (MFN) basis. Unfortunately, this form of protection is often likely to be ineffective during the lengthy period that the affected industry lobbies the government to restrict imports from one country after another as production expands in noncontrolled countries. Firms and workers are also likely to believe that protection will eventually work, and they tend to postpone the hard adjustment decisions they eventually must make.

These reactions have been documented by the International Trade Commission in the reports it makes on the effectiveness of previous protection when an industry requests the continuation of protection. A good example is the protection granted to the domestic color television industry in 1977 when the US government negotiated an OMA quantitatively limiting Japanese exports of color television receivers and subassemblies thereof to the United States to about 70 percent of Japan's 1976 level.

Exports of color television sets from Taiwan and Korea increased fourfold in 1977 and 1978 with their share of the US market rising from 1.5 percent in 1976 to 7.2 percent in 1978. Japan's share fell from 18.7 to 10.8 percent between these years but the import share from all sources only declined from 21.3 to 20.9 percent. Because this reaction to the protection rendered the program almost completely ineffective, the Carter administration negotiated OMAs with both Taiwan and Korea that became effective in 1979. The total import share dropped to 13.7 percent in 1979. But imports from Mexico and Singapore continued to rise during this period. These countries' share of imports of complete and incomplete color television receivers increased from 16 percent in 1976 to 37 percent in 1979, while the share of the countries covered by the OMAs fell from 82 to 59 percent between these years.

A significant increase in imports from noncontrolled countries also occurred when the US government negotiated OMAs with Taiwan and Korea in 1977, as a means to protect the domestic nonrubber footwear industry. While the volume of imported nonrubber footwear from Taiwan and Korea declined from 206 million pairs to 180 million pairs between 1977 and 1978, imports from other sources increased from 160 million pairs to 193 million pairs. As a consequence of the increase in imports from noncontrolled sources, the total US import share by volume increased from 47.0 percent in 1976, the last year before import restraints, to 51.0 percent in 1981, the last year of the restraint period, even though the import share of Taiwan and Korea fell from 25.4 to 22.0 percent between these years.

6 Conclusions

The history of US trade policy since World War II can be explained in political economy terms as a response both to changing world patterns of comparative advantage and to major political and economic shocks outside the trading sector. Trade-policy decisions in the early postwar period were shaped by the emergence of the United States from World War II as the dominant economic power among the market-oriented economies, and the political leader of the efforts to contain Soviet expansionism. A liberal American trade policy not only facilitated the economic recovery of other nations opposed to Soviet political expansion but, by leading to liberal trade policies on the part of other countries, enabled US exporters and investors to establish strong world market positions prior to the full economic recovery of those industrial competitors whose economies had been crippled during the war.

The outward-looking US policies were not only of great benefit to the United States, but helped to facilitate the highly successful recovery and modernization efforts in most industrial countries and in a number of developing nations. An understandable consequence, however, was that a growing list of labor-intensive or low-technology US industries, which had enjoyed artificially prosperous conditions in the early postwar years, began to face severe competitive pressure from foreign producers and, therefore, to lobby for import protection. The easing of the Cold War tensions also made it more difficult to resist these domestic pressures on the grounds that an open trade policy was needed to help strengthen the free world against communist expansion.

An effective argument used in lobbying for protection has been that unfair trade practices by other countries are a major cause of US competitive problems. It has the appeal of diverting attention from any domestic factors that might explain these problems, and of enabling public and private officials still to maintain that they favor free trade. They maintain that this trade must be fair as well as free, however. The importance of this view is indicated by the strong US emphasis on negotiating new codes of behavior on fair trade issues in the Tokyo Round. The United States and other industrial countries also began to direct their protective actions toward particular countries that they felt were unfairly disrupting domestic markets with sharp increases in exports.

The sharp dollar appreciation in the early 1980s adversely affected most export-oriented and import-competing industries and changed trade policy from being a matter of concern to only a small number of industries into being a matter of national concern. This development gave impetus to the view that unfair actions by foreigners adversely affected almost all industries and were a major cause of the massive US trade deficit. Emphasis shifted from the view that unfair foreign measures were a major cause of import surges to the view that these measures were a major cause of the failure of US exporters to sell more in foreign markets. Consequently, there has recently been a series of vigorous bilateral efforts by the administration to open the markets of Japan and a number of developing countries. Most members of Congress still believe the administration has not gone far enough along these lines and the new Omnibus Trade Act mandates an even tougher approach.

Although all countries are likely to benefit economically from more open markets, the United States may be paying an undesirable price in foreign policy terms for its aggressive behavior. The US advice to surplus countries, that greater emphasis on stimulating demand from domestic activities is needed, also may have undesirable long-run growth effects in the world economy, if import-substitution policies are given greater prominence in countries' growth efforts. Foreign market opportunities for US goods may be less favorable because of such policies. In addition, as the importance of an export surplus grows due to the increasing service charges required for the growing US net indebtedness position, the argument that fairness requires bilaterally balanced trade may be thrown back at the United States to thwart the achievement of such a surplus.

References

Balassa, Bela, 1986. Japan's trade policies, *Weltwirtschaftliches Archiv*, 122(4) December, 745–90.

Baldwin, Robert E., 1958. The commodity composition of trade: selected industrial countries, 1900–1954, *The Review of Economics and Statistics*, 40, 50–68.

Baldwin, Robert E., 1962. Implications of structural changes in commodity trade. In *Factors Affecting the United States Balance of Payments*, Part 1, Washington, DC: Joint Economic Committee, 87th Congress, 2nd Session.

Bergsten, C. Fred and Cline, William R., 1985. *The United States–Japan Economic Problem*, Washington, DC: Institute of International Economics.

Branson, W., 1980. Trends in U.S. international trade and investment since World War II. In *The American Economy in Transition*, Martin Feldstein (ed.), Chicago: University of Chicago Press and National Bureau of Economic Research.

Economic Report of the President, 1985. Washington, DC: US Government Printing Office.

Economic Report of the President, 1986. Washington, DC: US Government Printing Office.

Economic Report of the President, 1988. Washington, DC: US Government Printing Office.

Keohane, R. O., 1984. *After Hegemony: Cooperation and Discord in the World Political Economy*, Princeton, NJ: Princeton University Press.

Lawrence, Robert Z., 1987. Does Japan import too little: closed markets of closed minds?. Paper prepared for Brookings Panel on Economic Activity, Washington, DC, September 10.

Leamer, Edward E., 1988. Measures of openness. In *Trade Policy Issues and Empirical Analyses*, R. E. Baldwin (ed.), Chicago: University of Chicago Press and National Bureau of Economic Research.

Nogues, Julio J., Olechowski, Andrzej, and Winters, L. Alan, 1985. The extent of non-tariff barriers to industrial countries' imports. Discussion Paper, Report DRD115, Washington, DC: The World Bank.

Noland, Marcus, 1987. *An Econometric Model of the Volume of International Trade*, Institute of International Economics, Washington, DC.

Saxonhouse, Gary R., 1983. The micro- and macroeconomics of foreign sales to Japan. In William Cline (ed.), *Trade Policy for the 1980s*, Cambridge, MA: MIT Press.

Saxonhouse, Gary R., 1985. What's wrong with Japanese trade structure?. Seminar Discussion Paper 166, Research Seminar in International Economics, Ann Arbor, MI: University of Michigan.

United States Department of Commerce, 1985. *United States Trade: Performance in 1984 and Outlook*, Washington, DC: International Trade Administration, US Department of Commerce.

2

Free Trade, Fair Trade? The Reagan Record

*Charles S. Pearson**

Introduction

The Reagan administration took office in 1981 with a clearly articulated economic philosophy, the centerpiece of which was maximum reliance on private enterprise and the price system and minimal government involvement in the economy. The principal domestic strategy would be to press forward with deregulation, to cut taxes, and to roll back nonmilitary government expenditures. The international dimension of an economic philosophy of *laissez-faire* is free trade. Considering the strong ideological cast to the Reagan economic program, one might have expected a noticeable shift in US trade policy in areas where the executive has influence. It did not materialize.

In fact, the evidence suggests that the economic philosophy of the Reagan administration had no discernable effects on US trade policy. When measured against the criteria of *laissez-faire* the Reagan administration fell short. There were no tariff reductions of consequence. International markets were cartelized with the aid and encouragement of the administration. Agricultural exports, even exports to the "evil empire," were subsidized. Discrimination in trade was embraced as the new US policy. Economic sanctions were frequently employed to serve foreign policy interests.

But a pure *laissez-faire* trade policy is too extreme a test, even for Reaganomics. A liberal trade system accepts a modest role for government in trade. And it is the tenets of liberal trade, not free trade, that have guided US trade policy since the Trade Agreements Act of 1934. Yet even when measured against the less demanding criteria of liberal trade the Reagan administration also fell short – arguably, shorter than all other postwar administrations. The practice of US trade policy in the past eight years has been characterized by frequent rhetorical bows toward liberal trade and some actions that promote it, but has also displayed a ready acceptance of departures based on "political" or pragmatic considerations, and not on principle. In this respect the Reagan administration has been indistinguishable from its predecessors in the postwar era.

One of the two major trade-liberalizing initiatives – the Uruguay Round – was off to a rocky start, in part because of foreign indifference but in part because of administration insistence that the negotiations focus on areas that are new and problematic for the GATT but that promote rather narrow US commercial interests. These new areas are: trade in (some) services, protection of intellectual property rights, and trade-related investment performance requirements. The Reagan administration also negotiated a free trade agreement with Canada. In the long run, this may promote liberal trade. But free trade agreements increase discrimination in trade, and the agreement with Canada represents a sharp reversal in a 50-year US policy of supporting nondiscrimination and generally opposing preferential trade arrangements. And the special treatment in the agreement given to politically sensitive industries bears the hallmark of politics, not principle.

Ironically, although the Reagan trade policy fell short of the practice of liberal trade, it also fell short for those who would pursue more aggressive actions, including stronger retaliation against so-called foreign unfair trade practices and against countries that have bilateral trade surpluses with the United States. Thus Reagan's trade policy can be damned by both liberal traders and by the "neoprotectionists" whose fixation on "fair trade" leads them to applaud unilateral action by the United States backed by market closing threats, who care little for the principle of nondiscrimination, and who would refashion the concept of reciprocity into an aggressive policy tool.

Despite some continuities in trade policy in the 1980s, there are important differences with regard to outcomes. Trade policy has become partially re-politicized along party lines, as it was during most of our pre-World War II history. Presidential influence over Congress in trade policy has weakened. The president's veto of the initial 1988 trade bill, followed by his signature of almost identical legislation shortly thereafter, illustrates the collapse of a bipartisan trade policy and the discord between the president and Congress. Domestic support for liberal trade has eroded and international trade disputes have become more intense and bitter. The United States may have become more protectionist, although the distinction between protectionist pressure, which has surely increased, and protectionist action, which is notoriously difficult to measure, must be kept in mind. Perhaps most important, the notion that world trade is "unfair" to the United States, and that the United States has the right and the duty to impose on others its standards of fair trade, has gained respectability and has become a cornerstone of US trade policy.

The apparent drift away from the bench mark of liberal trade toward protection during the Reagan years suggests two competing explanations. The first is that the Reagan administration bears major responsibility through its own actions, through its inability to influence others, especially Congress, and through inattention. This interpretation suggests that trade policy performance under Reagan was indifferent or poor.

An alternative interpretation is that the environment in which the Reagan administration found itself was hostile to liberal trade. In this view, adverse macroeconomic factors – a recession early in the first term, massive trade deficits, and sluggish world economic growth – and longer-term structural forces undermining the role of the president in trade policy and altering the competitive position of the United States in the world economy, were responsible for the drift away from liberal trade. In this interpretation, the administration waged a praiseworthy and generally successful holding action. While making some tactical concessions, its aggressive actions to open foreign markets and its leadership in launching the Uruguay Round of trade negotiations laid the groundwork for further trade liberalization. And it held at bay strong protectionist forces within Congress.

One purpose of this paper is to investigate whether *laissez-faire* economic philosophy influenced the conduct of trade policy under Reagan, and to examine whether (and why) there was backsliding in the practice of liberal trade policy. At a different level, the paper assesses the forces and trends that brought trade issues to such prominence in recent years, and the implications for the Bush administration.

Too often, debate on US trade policy neglects its own rich history, especially the long period before liberal trade became the prevailing dogma. Accordingly, the first section recalls some of the antecedents to the current trade policy debate and suggests that the United States may be reverting to its nineteenth century trade policies, discarded earlier in this century. The second section analyzes trade performance in the Reagan years in five areas – import protection (liberalization), discrimination, reciprocity, subvention of exports, and the use of trade policy to secure other foreign policy objectives. The final section discusses some underlying forces in US trade policy and draws conclusions.

Historical perspective

Although often ignored, trade issues have a rich history, and a glance back is revealing. Most of the so-called modern questions of trade policy debated during the Reagan years – trade in services, protection of intellectual property rights, foreign unfair trade practices, aggressive reciprocity, relations between Congress and the president – have roots deep in the history of US commercial policy. Moreover, the principal tenets of a liberal trade policy – resisting import protection, nondiscrimination, reciprocity in trade concessions, resisting the use of trade for foreign policy goals – were actively debated in the nineteenth century.

It appears that the United States under President Reagan partly reverted to commercial practices that in many respects resembled its policy in the nineteenth and early twentieth centuries, a policy characterized by periodic bouts of protectionism, discrimination, bargaining over tariffs, and domestic politicization of trade.

Protection arguments

Consider, for example, protection. The US commitment to unrestricted imports has been anything but steadfast. The first tariff act (1789) had elements of protection, but of a modest nature, and was mainly for revenue purposes. Preference was given to American ships in the coastwise trade, protection that survives to this day. American trade at the time thrived on agricultural exports, *entrepôt* trade, and shipping services.[1] The comparative advantage in agriculture and services that the United States is currently alleged to have thus replicates a pattern that existed much earlier, i.e. before manufactures became dominant. The situation changed abruptly with the Embargo Act of 1807, the Non-Intercourse Act of 1809, and the subsequent War of 1812.[2] Tariff rates were doubled during the war and import-substituting manufacturing was greatly stimulated.

Industries that had sprung up during and after the war (e.g. cotton and woolen manufactures and iron manufactures) pressed for protection when normal conditions of trade returned and the price of imported manufactures fell. The infant industry argument for protection was widely used, and when it was no longer plausible with maturing industries, the pauper labor argument became attractive. By and large, domestic producers were successful at seeking increased duties, with successive tariff acts increasing the level of protection, starting in 1816 and culminating in the highly protective Tariff Act of 1828, the "Tariff of Abominations" (opposed by shipping and merchant interests in New England and by agricultural interests in the South). Protection declined irregularly after 1828 until the revenue needs of the Civil War again led to greatly increased tariff rates, which remained in force long after the war.

World War I contributed to another bout of protectionism. Although no tariff act was passed during hostilities, as revenue needs were met by income and excise taxes, the disruption of trade again stimulated new branches of manufacturing. When the Republican party regained power in 1920, these so-called "war babies" claimed protection. National security justifications, especially in branches of the chemical industry, were trotted out. The result, the Tariff Act of 1922, returned tariff rates to extremely protective levels. Even these were surpassed by the infamous Smoot-Hawley tariff of 1930.

Thus the current protectionist climate in Congress and the national debate on trade repeats earlier cycles. Nor are the principal arguments – infant industry, national security, pauper labor, protection of employment and wages – new, although they must be dressed up for the modern citizen. One cloak that is now widely used is the call for "fair trade" and a "level playing field." But even that cloak has been worn before.

The most outrageous variation of the level playing field proposition was the so-called "true principle" of protection for determining the "scientific" tariff, first put forward in the Republican platform of 1908[3] in the following terms:

> In all protective legislation the true principle of protection is best maintained by the imposition of such duties as will equal the difference between the cost of production at home and abroad, together with a reasonable profit to American industries.

This most unscientific of principles was only slightly modified in 1913 when the Democrats proposed that the guiding principle should be a "competitive tariff," one that allows the domestic producer to compete on even terms with the foreign producer. That strict application of this principle would end in full autarky did not prevent the newly established United States Tariff Board from making laborious, if probably inaccurate, estimates of foreign and domestic production costs, and did not prevent the House Ways and Means Committee from considering production cost differentials in setting tariff rates. Incidentally, the US tariff system had long been cognizant of the effective rate of protection on value added and so, for example, in calculating the scientific tariff for woolen goods at 35 percent in the 1913 tariff, the simultaneous elimination of duties on wool was taken into account.[4] The practical difficulties of determining foreign production costs still plague US antidumping and countervailing duty cases.

Unfair trade and reciprocity

Concern for foreign unfair trade practices, apart from the irrational "scientific tariff" argument, also dots US commercial history. Both the Tariff Act of 1890 and the Tariff Act of 1897 authorized the president to impose duties on certain imports if in his judgement the exporting country imposed duties or other extractions which he deemed reciprocally unreasonable or unjust. This foreshadowed section 301 of the Trade Act of 1974, which authorized import restrictions against foreign trade practices deemed unreasonable, unjustifiable, or discriminatory.

The Tariff Act of 1909 also foreshadowed section 301 (of the 1974 Trade Act), although it came to little in the end. A penalty tariff of 25 percent *ad valorem* was to be added to minimum *ad valorem* rates and applied to countries which "unduly discriminate" against the United States. The scope was very broad, to include discrimination "in the way of tariff rates or provisions, trade or other regulations, charges, exactions, or in any other manner," or by export bounty or export duty.[5] Negotiations were conducted with Germany, France, and Canada, and some minor adjustments were made by them, so that in the end President Taft could conclude that he was satisfied no country unduly discriminated against the United States. This was an easy decision to take for, unlike today, the political climate was moving against protection.[6]

The related concepts of reciprocity and nondiscrimination also are deeply woven into US commercial policy history and underlie current trade issues such as the recent US pursuit of free trade agreements and unilateral preferential agreements (Caribbean Basin Initiative, 1983; US–Israel Free-Trade Agreement, 1984; US–Canada Free-Trade Agreement, 1987), the use of section 301, the "graduation" of the "Gang of Four" (Taiwan, South Korea, Hong Kong, Singapore) from the Generalized System of Preferences in 1988, and the telecommunications provisions of the 1988 omnibus trade bill.[7]

Reciprocity in US commercial treaties resulting in discrimination (i.e., the failure to free up trade through unconditional most favored nation status) did not start with the free trade agreements with Israel and Canada in the 1980s. The Treaty of 1854 with Great Britain permitted duty-free trade in a number of agricultural products between the United States and Canada and was thus discriminatory.[8] Also, foreshadowing the US–Israel free trade agreement, political objectives led to US reciprocity treaties with Hawaii (1875) and Cuba (1903). Preferential access for Hawaiian sugar and the consequent financial windfall to the planter class led to peaceful annexation of the islands by the United States in 1898. Preferential status and windfalls in sugar also accrued to Cuba, but for better or worse there was no annexation. Reciprocity treaties were negotiated with thirteen other countries during the period 1844–99, but in general failed to obtain Senate ratification. They failed, not because of any sensitivity to their discriminatory character, but because protectionist interests in the United States were opposed to duty-free imports and objected.

Improving export market access, either to remove foreign discrimination or to secure preferential treatment, was the principal motivation for the US pursuit of reciprocity.[9] But the argument then, as today, was frequently garbed in appeals to fair trade. Thus the protectionist secretary of state, James Blaine, cleverly appealed to notions of fairness in seeking concessions

UNIVERSITY
OF BRISTOL
LIBRARY
WITHDRAWN

in Latin America: "It was the application of the golden rule of commerce – the doctrine of fair trade – to insist that the countries whose products had so long been admitted free to our parts should admit our products free to theirs."[10] Blaine neglected to mention that US imports from Latin America were raw materials and food, mainly noncompetitive with US production, and that Latin America did not discriminate between imports from the United States and Europe. In 1890 the countries of Latin America turned down a proposed customs union with the United States on the sensible ground that Europe, which supplied Latin America with 90 percent of its imports, would not look kindly on overt tariff discrimination.

It is interesting to note that in the second half of the nineteenth century, Britain's free trade policy, in effect for some 50 years, came under attack for failing to demand reciprocity from trade partners. Many of the arguments for abandoning unilateral free trade and practicing aggressive reciprocity were then, as today in the United States, couched in terms of fair trade, and organizations such as the National Fair Trade League and the Reciprocity Free Trade Association were active. Ultimately, the fair trade movement failed in Britain as it did not receive support from labor, consumers, and other groups.[11]

In the nineteenth century, mutual exchange of trade concessions between the United States and other countries was a source of bitter dispute in those instances where the United States had most favored nation (MFN) clauses in commercial treaties with third countries. For a century and a half, until 1923, the United States took the position that an MFN clause was conditional. So insistent was the United States that this became known as the American interpretation. For example, the United States had had, since 1826, a commercial treaty with Denmark incorporating an MFN clause, but when Hawaiian sugar was admitted duty-free in 1875, the Supreme Court ruled that equal treatment need not be applied to sugar from the Danish island of St Croix. The conditional interpretation of the MFN clause was finally reversed in 1923, when it became apparent that US export interests had much to gain from an unconditional worldwide MFN policy. The concept of conditional MFN status, however, finds strong echoes in the codes negotiated in the Tokyo Round of tariff negotiations, which make certain benefits (e.g. requirement for an injury test in US countervailing cases) contingent on the foreign country signing the particular code. Thus conditional MFN status has re-emerged in the area of nontariff barrier and unfair trade regulations. It will surely surface again if and when an agreement on services is reached in the Uruguay Round.

The concept of reciprocity is closely linked to the MFN concept. From the 1934 Reciprocal Trade Act until recently, reciprocity in trade negotiations meant that all parties received roughly equivalent "concessions." A quite different meaning of reciprocity has emerged in recent years.[12] This new or "aggressive" reciprocity seeks equivalence in export market access between the United States and other countries, and thus is basically bilateral in character. Moreover, it is generally sector- or product-specific, i.e. providing equivalent access on a product-by-product, country-by-country basis. It also differs from the conventional GATT meaning of reciprocity in concessions following multilateral trade negotiations in that it is employed unilaterally by the United States to overcome foreign trade barriers, and is backed up by the threat of trade retaliation. Finally, because the concept is applied bilaterally and often focuses on outcomes rather than protection levels, it can easily slide into demands for bilateral trade balancing, either overall or product by product.

This new meaning of reciprocity (equivalent market access, country by country and product by product) has no strong direct roots in US commercial history. It emerged in the late 1970s and early 1980s as a response to perceived unequal access and unfair trade practices, most notably by Japan. It did not originate primarily as an administration initiative but in a series of Congressional bills designed to achieve a "level playing field."[13]

A final historical point involves the changing relation between Congress and the president in making trade policy. The dramatic turning point was the Trade Act of 1934. Up to that time Congress had delegated to the president concrete but quite limited powers, for example, the power to impose countervailing and antidumping duties, and limited power to use concessions and penalty tariffs for bargaining purposes. The 1934 act not only granted the president the authority to reduce tariffs by up to 50 percent in exchange for reciprocal reductions, but got Congress out of the business of setting tariff rates product by product.[14] The conventional interpretation is that Congress was dismayed by its own ineptitude in passing the Smoot-Hawley tariff, and wished to protect itself from direct political pressures it could not handle.[15] Since then, Congress and the president have struggled over control of trade policy, and the struggle became open and intense during the Reagan years.

To summarize, during the period between 1923, when the United States abandoned conditional MFN policy, and 1934, when the Trade Act of 1934 was passed, the United States moved decisively away from the commercial policy of a weak state unsure of competitive strength. By and large, it gave up reciprocity treaties, bargaining tariffs, special deals, conditional MFN status, and so forth. It actively promoted unconditional MFN policy as the central principle of the GATT, and only reluctantly accepted customs unions as a limited exception. Starting in 1934 and continuing after World War II, the United States followed through on its commitment to remove high protective tariffs. An attempt was made, with only partial success, to depoliticize trade by transferring trade authority from Congress to the president. The call for fair trade was muted. Yet this shift has not proved permanent. In important respects, trade policy actions in the Reagan years were reminiscent of US commercial policy in the nineteenth and early twentieth centuries. This "backsliding" is examined next.

Trade policy performance

The absence of *any* government actions to promote or restrict trade is a good, simple test of a strong commitment to *laissez-faire*. Testing the commitment to liberal trade is more difficult. The elements of a liberal trade policy are resistance to import restrictions, export subsidies and export restraints, the use of MFN tariffs when import protection is (reluctantly) employed, nondiscrimination among trade partners, adherence to the traditional concept of reciprocity in trade negotiations, and a sparing use of trade measures to secure foreign policy objectives. Thus liberal trade is a matter of degree and not absolutes.

Import restrictions

Escape clause and market disruption Although narrow in scope, escape clause cases give perhaps the clearest evidence of executive tilt for or against protection. Escape clause causes do not involve allegations of unfair trade, and thus skirt the vexed question of whether antidumping and countervailing duties are truly protection or merely measures to correct market distortions. Moreover, US trade law gives the president a direct role in the escape clause proceedings. After a positive injury finding and a remedy recommendation by the International Trade Commission (ITC), the president must decide, after considering broader aspects of the national interest, whether to protect the industry, offer adjustment assistance, or do nothing.

Seven escape clause cases with positive ITC recommendations for protection reached the president between 1981 and 1988. The seven cases involved canned mushrooms, heavyweight motorcycles, stainless and alloy steel, carbon and alloy steel, unwrought copper, nonrubber footwear, and wood shakes and shingles. Protection was granted for mushrooms, motorcycles, stainless steel, and wood shakes and shingles. In related escape clause actions, the president turned down a recommended extension of protection of nonrubber footwear in 1981, but extended protection of stainless steel in 1987. Thus of the seven original cases, President Reagan provided increased protection in four although not necessarily in the form and amount recommended by the ITC. In the key case of carbon and alloy steel the president rejected escape clause relief, but turned around and ordered the negotiation of restrictive market sharing agreements involving quantitative limits with all major exporters. Inclusion of steel brings the number of protectionist actions up to five. This compares with seven of 17 cases with positive ITC recommendations in which protection was granted during the Carter presidency.

Of the five instances of escape clause protection in the Reagan years (including carbon and alloy steel), two involved the imposition of MFN tariffs, the third (heavyweight motorcycles) involved a tariff-rate quota, with quotas set by country of origin, the fourth (stainless steel) involved a combination of tariffs and quotas, and the fifth (carbon and alloy steel) involved country-specific quotas. Of the seven cases in the Carter years, tariffs were used in four, quotas in one, and orderly marketing agreements (OMAs) in two (the OMA is a bilateral, quantitative restraint). Liberal trade tenets generally support MFN tariffs over other instruments.

Although less frequently used than the escape clause, section 406 of the Trade Act of 1974 can also test the president's tilt toward liberal trade or protection, as he has an explicit role in deciding whether to accept or reject an ITC recommendation. Cases under section 406 involve the question of whether market disruption exists as a result of imports from a communist country. There were two positive findings by the ITC during the Carter years and both were rejected by him. President Reagan also faced two cases. He received a split decision from the ITC with respect to canned mushrooms from the People's Republic of China (PRC) and chose to determine that market disruption did not exist. With ammonium paratungstate and tungstic acid for the PRC, he accepted the ITC finding and negotiated an OMA.

Exclusive focus on escape clause and market disruption cases as a litmus test for protection can be misleading. The industries seeking relief differ greatly in size. For example, the US clothespin industry with 387 workers, which received protection from the Carter administration, is not equivalent to the nonrubber footwear industry with 150,000 workers, which failed to receive protection from President Reagan in 1985. Moreover, protectionists can make an end run around the escape clause. Industries can receive protection through the so-called unfair trade laws (antidumping and countervailing duty), by appealing directly to Congress, or by engineering foreign "voluntary export restraint" (VER) agreements.

The Reagan administration was involved in nine cases in which major domestic industries sought increased protection. The industries were autos, nonrubber footwear, textiles and apparel, sugar, machine tools, steel, softwood lumber, copper, and semiconductors. The combined 1987 import value for these industries exceeded $100 billion. The semiconductor case is considered separately below. Three of the remaining eight cases were fair trade cases and were considered initially through the escape clause (autos, footwear, copper). Two cases involved allegations of unfair trade, either dumping, subsidies, or both (steel and lumber). In the case of steel, escape clause protection was also sought. Textiles and apparel fell under the Multifiber Arrangement (MFA), sugar was protected under section 22 of the Agricultural Adjustment Act, and machine tool imports were ultimately considered within the national security provisions of the trade law. Six of the eight industries received additional protection; footwear and copper did not. A brief review provides some insight into the Reagan trade philosophy.

Automobiles The case of automobiles is especially instructive. During the last year of the Carter administration United Auto Workers (UAW) president Douglas Fraser unsuccessfully requested Japanese auto makers to voluntarily limit their exports to the United States. Failing in this, the UAW and Ford took their cases directly to Congress, requesting domestic content legislation and suggesting that the Carter administration negotiate an OMA with Japan to limit auto exports. The Carter administration's position was that domestic content legislation would circumvent US and GATT escape clause procedures and that the president did not have the authority to negotiate an OMA without a positive injury finding by the ITC. Failing to secure direct presidential or Congressional action, the UAW and Ford filed an escape clause petition with the ITC seeking tariff and quota relief. In November 1980 the ITC rejected the petition, voting three to two that imports were not a substantial cause of serious injury. A decline in demand associated with recession, and the shift to small, fuel efficient cars, induced by gas prices, were found to be more important.[16]

Autos were thus the first big trade decision confronting the Reagan administration in early 1981. During the 1980 election campaign, Reagan had traveled to Detroit and promised assistance to the auto industry.[17] Pressure on Congress resumed in early 1981 and Senators Danforth and Bentsen introduced highly restrictive quota legislation directed against Japan. The Reagan administration officials thus had a clear choice, and one that because of its high visibility could set the tone for trade policy for the duration. They could lobby against the quota legislation, and if it passed Congress, the president could veto it, or they could yield on principle and pressure Japan into "voluntary" restraint. Coming early in his term and involving a major domestic industry, it was a strategic decision. In opposing the legislation it would have been easy to cite the recent ITC decision; if a veto were overridden, opposition to the legislation would still have served to establish presidential commitment to liberal trade, and respect for established escape clause procedures. In the end, the choice was to push Japan toward so-called voluntary export restraints (VERs), and after some mixed signals, principally concerning acceptable levels of quotas, Japan acceded.[18]

The lesson from autos is that a major domestic industry, when denied relief under existing legislation, could turn to the government for irregular protection. The president, wishing to reduce and deflect political pressure, granted the industry protection, using a trade device that is both discriminatory and outside GATT procedures and that diminished the established escape clause procedures, but that offered a thin patina of free trade respectability by placing the immediate onus for trade restriction on Japan. It is impossible to discern a commitment to *laissez-faire* or liberal trade in this action.

Footwear The case of nonrubber footwear has a different ending and provides the most telling evidence in support of a liberal trade cast on the part of the Reagan administration. In 1977 the ITC found that increased imports were a significant cause of serious injury, and recommended import relief in the form of tariff quotas. President Carter chose to negotiate OMAs with two rapidly growing major suppliers of low priced shoes, Taiwan and South Korea, setting a precedent for illiberal and discriminatory relief. In early 1981 the domestic industry petitioned for extension of relief and the ITC recommended termination of the OMA with Korea and liberalized extension of the OMA with Taiwan. President Reagan, in the summer of 1981, chose not to extend either OMA. One can speculate that the motive was to refurbish free trade credentials, tarnished by the Japanese VER in autos several months earlier.

In 1984 the domestic footwear industry filed another escape clause petition which was denied by the ITC on the ground that the industry as a whole was not suffering serious injury. The Senate Finance Committee was not happy with the decision and requested reinvestigation before the customary one year had elapsed, partly on the ground that marginal changes made in the 1984 Trade Act altered the criteria for finding serious injury. The ITC reversed itself in June 1985, unanimously finding injury and voting four to one for auctioned import quotas on nonrubber footwear from all sources. The European Community (EC) and other suppliers threatened retaliation, and President Reagan, citing the cost of protection to consumers, rejected trade restraints and ordered an adjustment and retraining program for footwear workers.

Rejecting the ITC's recommendation for protection of the footwear industry was politically expensive for the president. The cost was particularly high as it came at a time when he was under strong attack for failing to have a trade policy that defended US interests.

Multifiber arrangement The United States has bilateral restraint agreements under the MFA with 34 countries, and by the mid-1980s some 80 percent of textile and apparel imports from developing countries were under quotas.[19] As early as the 1980 campaign, candidate Reagan had written to Senator Strom Thurmond of South Carolina, pledging to strengthen the MFA when it came up for renewal in 1981. This was followed in 1983 by unilateral imposition of quotas against the PRC by the Reagan administration and retaliation by the PRC against US agricultural exports. Again in 1983, the US industry initiated a countervailing duty petition against the PRC and, partly in response, President Reagan overruled a majority of his Cabinet and tightened enforcement of the quotas against low-cost suppliers. The Department of Commerce also tightened rules of origin in 1985, with a further slight increase in the level of protection.[20]

The administration found itself in a difficult position in the period leading up to the July 1986 MFA renewal. In late 1985 the Jenkins bill rolling back imports of textiles and apparel (and restricting copper and footwear imports) had passed both House and Senate by large margins. In December 1985 President Reagan vetoed the bill, but the veto override vote was deliberately set for the following summer to put maximum pressure on the administration to toughen the terms for MFA-IV (forth multi-fibre arrangement) negotiations and to negotiate more restrictive bilateral quotas with principal suppliers. The strategy was successful. Three important and more restrictive bilateral agreements with Hong Kong, Taiwan, and Korea were reached in summer 1986, and MFA-IV itself was made more restrictive rather than more liberal.[21]

Sugar Sugar is another product with a long history of protection, dating to the tariff of 1789, although until about 1880 the tariff was designed for revenue purposes and only later to protect Louisiana sugar cane producers. In May 1977 President Carter rejected an ITC escape clause recommendation for quotas on sugar imports, and instituted direct income payments to match the differential between market prices and a domestic target price. Falling world prices subsequently led him to increase the tariff and impose an import fee. The Reagan administration initially opposed inclusion of sugar in the 1981 farm bill, but subsequently withdrew opposition to obtain support from Louisiana representatives for its omnibus budget-cutting resolution.[22] To meet the domestic price targets of the 1981 act without budget cost, President Reagan first raised the tariff to its statutory ceiling and imposed additional fees. The import fee was subsequently scrapped by the Reagan administration and replaced with an import quota scheme designed to secure the domestic price target, although the higher tariff was retained. In January 1985 President Reagan, by emergency proclamation, placed quotas on a number of food products containing sugar (e.g. pancake mix) because of the suspicion that sugar was being "smuggled" into the United States through prepared food products and later extracted and sold at the high protected US price.[23] The import quota on sugar has been successively tightened, from 3 million tons in 1984 to 750,000 tons in 1988.

Sugar was explicitly excluded from the Caribbean Basin Initiative. Although Congress must surely share responsibility, there is nothing in the Reagan record on sugar that hints of liberal trade principles.

National security: machine tools In May 1982 a US manufacturer, Houdaille Industries, sought import relief through a novel channel, a provision of the Revenue Act of 1971. This provision allows exclusion of imported machines from the investment tax credit program if the country of origin engages in certain unfair trade practices. Houdaille alleged that Japan practiced unfair trade in machine tools. In April 1983 the president decided against action (overruling Commerce Secretary Baldridge and United States Trade Representative Brock, who favored a finding of unfairness, and negotiations with Japan).[24]

In the interim (in March 1983), the United States National Machine Tool Builders Association had petitioned for import relief under the national security clause (section 232 of the Trade Act of 1962). This time around, in a deteriorating climate for liberal trade and following creation by the administration of a trade strike force in the fall of 1985, the Commerce Department determined that imports of machine tools presented a threat to national security. In May 1986, President Reagan directed that "voluntary export restraint" agreements be negotiated with Japan, Taiwan, Switzerland, and West Germany. Japan and Taiwan capitulated and agreed to roll back their share of US consumption to 1981 and 1985 levels, depending on machine tool category. Both countries agreed to control exports through licensing schemes. Germany and Switzerland did not roll over so easily, and in the end President Reagan simply ordered that imports of machine tools from these two countries not exceed specific quantitative limits. In addition he informed other supplying countries not to increase their market share, and he imposed an import monitoring system. Interestingly, the government claims that this series of actions does not constitute the use of section 232 authority.[25] What was initially an alleged unfair trade case (albeit through a novel channel) became widespread protection, of a discriminatory character, on the grounds of national security.

Cartelizing steel Steel has had more or less continuous special protection since 1969.[26] The first phase, from 1969 to 1974, involved so-called voluntary export restraints by Japan and the EC. The second phase was from 1977 to 1982 when, as initiated by President Carter, the United States set floor prices for imported steel based on Japanese production costs, creating a "trigger price mechanism." This was done to head off numerous unfair trade petitions. The third phase started in 1982 when the industry filed massive new countervailing duty and antidumping petitions. Despite the fact that the Department of Commerce found few if any subsidies for a significant portion of imports from the EC, thus providing the Reagan administration with an unseized opportunity to reject protection, Secretary of Commerce Baldridge negotiated a protective market sharing agreement with the EC.[27] The final phase started in 1984 when an industry-sponsored escape clause petition succeeded before the ITC by a three-to-two vote. Although President Reagan rejected the escape clause relief, he promptly directed the USTR to negotiate "voluntary export restraints" with all significant suppliers with a view to reducing imports to 18.5 percent of domestic consumption. The United States now has agreements with 19 countries and the EC. The agreements take the form of market share limitations and quotas, thus effectively cartelizing steel trade and granting the US industry substantial new protection.[28] There is nothing in the steel record of the Reagan administration that hints of liberal trade.

Upstream subsidies: lumber Softwood lumber imports from Canada were another important and contentious trade issue in the Reagan administration. The economic, legal, and political elements of the case are complex, but need only be briefly summarized here.[29] By 1982 imports of Canadian soft-wood lumber had captured 29 percent of US consumption. Production of US lumber, in the midst of a housing slump, was down 26 percent from its 1978 peak. A US lumber products lobby filed a countervailing duty petition with the Department of Commerce in October 1982 but was denied relief in May 1983 when the International Trade Administration of the US Department of Commerce rejected the argument that low Canadian stumpage fees were subsidies against which countervailing duties could be applied, and thus the remaining total of Canadian subsidies was *de minimis*. Meanwhile, a 1984 trade bill under consideration by Congress contained a provision which extended the right to apply countervailing duties to subsidized natural resource inputs (the upstream subsidy issue), but the White House resisted the provision and it was dropped. In March 1985 Secretary of Commerce Baldridge reconfirmed the commitment of the administration to the 1983 ITA finding, denying relief.

The issue did not die, however. In early 1986 the administration suggested talks with Canada on softwood lumber to be carried out through the USTR on the American side, and after a lapse the talks were resumed in January 1986 against a backdrop of rising protectionist sentiment in Congress and the earlier introduction of a large number of protectionist bills dealing with natural resources subsidies or, more directly, with softwood lumber imports. Eager to obtain Senate Finance Committee support for a free trade agreement with Canada, President Reagan promised in a public letter to committee chairman Robert Packwood that he would resolve the softwood lumber issue before concluding a free trade agreement with Canada.[30]

The administration's reversal of support for the ITA's 1983 decision, plus alleged changes in the interpretation of US countervailing duty laws, encouraged the US lumber industry to file a second countervailing duty petition in May 1986, but not before the administration attempted direct bilateral negotiations outside the legal procedures of the countervailing duty statutes. The negotiations failed in large part because the US lumber lobby found the initial Canadian offer unattractive. However, bilateral talks between Canada and the USTR looking for a negotiated solution continued during the new ITA investigation.

In the end, the ITA, in October 1986, reversed its 1983 decision and found that Canadian stumpage fees were a subsidy which could be countervailed and that the total Canadian subsidy amounted to 15 percent. In the period before the countervailing duty was to go into effect, Canada announced a retaliatory 70 percent duty on imports of US corn. Rather than let the countervailing duty stand, the administration reached an agreement with Canada (and apparently with the US lumber lobby) under which Canada could, rather than face the US tariff, impose a 15 percent discriminatory export tax on softwood lumber exports to the United States. In this fashion the Reagan administration managed to negotiate an agreement that raised the cost of lumber an estimated $1,000 per house and gave the windfall back to Canada in the form of an export tariff. Moreover, it did so by means of an export tariff that discriminated against the United States and was a reversal of its earlier firm rejection of countervailing natural resource input subsidies. Finally, the agreement was reached outside normal countervailing duty channels and permitted the domestic industry to essentially have veto power. Politics, not liberal trade principles, were the hallmark.

Copper US copper producers petitioned for escape clause relief in 1984 and the ITC, finding injury, came to a split recommendation for relief: two members proposed quotas and two proposed tariffs. Copper fabricators in the United States mounted a strong antiprotection campaign, pointing out that downstream copper-using industries, offering several times the employment of the mines, would be damaged. President Reagan agreed and denied relief on the grounds that it would not be in the US national interest. In particular, the harm that would be done to downstream copper fabricators was cited, together with the harm that would be done to heavily indebted copper exporting countries.[31]

To summarize, the record of the Reagan administration in resisting new import protection was weak. Six of the eight major industries gained additional protection (autos, textiles and apparel, steel, softwood lumber, machine tools, and sugar), all of these receiving relief through discriminatory (non-MFN) measures, and five of the six through quantitative restrictions (autos, textiles, steel, machine tools, and sugar). Only the 1985 denial of relief to the nonrubber footwear industry was a politically costly decision that conformed to liberal trade principles, although even then the industry was left with substantial protection.

Nondiscrimination

The Reagan administration's performance with respect to nondiscrimination can be examined in three areas: discrimination in new protection, discrimination through preferential and free trade agreements, and discrimination incidental to the pursuit of export market access.

New protection The evidence is mixed with regard to new protection obtained through the escape clause. Of the four cases in which the president offered trade relief, two involved an increase in MFN tariffs and one (stainless steel) the establishment of country-specific quotas. In the case of heavyweight motorcycles, the president established a tariff-rate quota system with country-specific quotas for Germany, for Japan, and for all other countries combined. In one of the two MFN tariff cases (wood shakes and shingles) 99 percent of imports were from Canada and thus, de facto, the burden of the US tariff was placed on a single exporter.

The evidence is less favorable with respect to new protection outside the escape clause. As previously described, increased trade restrictions in autos, textiles, sugar, softwood lumber, machine tools, and steel were all of a discriminatory nature, although it must be acknowledged that President Reagan was not the first to use discriminatory protection in textiles, sugar and steel, and softwood lumber, as a countervailing duty case necessarily involves non-MFN trade restraints.

International rules concerning discrimination in escape clause actions have been a matter of contention since the Tokyo Round in the 1970s. The US position, carried over now to the Uruguay Round, is that, in general, safeguard actions should be taken on an MFN basis, but some departure would be acceptable if they helped bring errant bilateral deals back within GATT rules and procedures. This official position has not kept the United States from applying numerous non-MFN import restraints.

Preferential trade The United States, under President Reagan, also experienced a revival of discrimination via free trade and preferential agreements, namely the Caribbean Basin Initiative (1983), the US–Israel Free-Trade Agreement (1984), and the US–Canada Free-Trade Agreement (1987). Foreign policy considerations probably dominated the first two agreements, although the US–Israel agreement also reflected frustration with the 1982 GATT ministerial meeting, and was also designed to neutralize any US disadvantage from an earlier preferential agreement between Israel and the EC. The US–Canadian agreement is substantially more important in economic terms. With two-way trade in goods and services exceeding $166 billion, the agreement represents a major increase in world trade conducted under non-MFN terms.

The provisions with respect to automobiles are particularly troubling. Under the US–Canadian auto pact, negotiated in 1965, the United States grants duty free access to the US market for cars and parts from Canada, provided they have a 50 percent North American content. For Canadians, interested in maintaining Canadian employment and output, the pact stipulated that imports from all sources were duty-free provided that the manufacturer maintained an agreed ratio of Canadian production of cars to Canadian sales of cars. In addition, Canada has a duty remission scheme that allows a dollar-for-dollar offset, for autos and auto parts purchased or made in Canada and exported, to be applied against duties on foreign cars imported into Canada. This scheme acts as an export subsidy for Japanese manufacturers operating in Canada and exporting to the United States. Under the new arrangements, the duty remissions will ultimately be phased out, a desirable outcome. But less happily, the benefits of the free trade accord are limited to the present participating manufacturers plus a General Motors – Suzuki joint venture. Thus new foreign manufacturers who establish production facilities in Canada will not be eligible to benefit. Present members, predominantly US firms but also including Volvo, will be able to qualify for duty-free imports into Canada from third countries. The big three US-based auto manufacturers currently import about $3 billion into Canada from third countries, and with a 9.2 percent Canadian import tariff, they can continue to save about $300 million in duties.[32] It follows that under the new arrangement, not only is there preferential (discriminatory) access to the US market, which has long existed, but a new discrimination has been established in favor of existing pact members, mainly US firms, and against new entrants. Moreover, the new free trade agreement toughened the 50 percent rule of origin for entry into the United States by basing it on manufacturing costs instead of value added, thus giving additional protection to North American manufacturers.

One could argue that despite selective provisions, the US–Canadian agreement provides a stimulus to global trade liberalization, as intended by the framers of the GATT when they authorized the customs union exemption to MFN policy. Moreover, the agreement contains provisions for freeing up trade in services and for limiting trade-related investment performance requirements, and thus may serve as something of a model for agreement in these areas in the Uruguay Round. It is at least arguable that these US initiatives toward preferential and free trade agreements (and our announced willingness to consider others) may prove to be the most effective strategy for trade liberalization in the current protectionist climate.

Nevertheless, it is remarkable that the principle of MFN status and nondiscrimination appears to have given no pause for the Reagan administration in its pursuit of these agreements. Since 1923, the United States has supported unconditional MFN status in its commercial treaties.[33] The extension of unconditional MFN treatment to countries that did not discriminate against the United States was central to the Trade Agreements Act of 1934 and was the major strategy for dealing with the proliferation of preferential trade agreements and bilateral trade balancing schemes that had sprung up after the Great Crash of 1929. The only preferential arrangements the United States entered into between that time and the US–Israel Free Trade Agreement were the US–Canadian auto pact of 1965 (a defensive move to forestall a trade dispute over subsidies) and our reluctant acceptance of the General Scheme of Preferences (GSP) for developing countries.

Thus the three preferential agreements initiated by the Reagan administration, and the invitation for other countries to negotiate similar agreements, represent a historic shift in US policy regarding MFN status and nondiscrimination. They represent a decisive turn away from liberal trade as it is conventionally understood.

Market access Trade discrimination occurs not only by differential treatment of imports but also by pressuring or cajoling preferential access to foreign markets, and therefore overlaps with the new meaning of reciprocity. The US–Japanese semiconductor agreement of July 1986 and the subsequent alleged noncompliance by Japan raise the issue of preferential access for the United States in the Japanese market. The semiconductor agreement was designed to meet US industry demands that Japan stop alleged dumping in the United States and third country markets and open its own market to foreign suppliers. In return, the United States government would suspend pending antidumping cases and a section 301 investigation. The market access commitment sought from Japan is an example of what Bhagwati and Irwin have called "voluntary import expansions" (VIEs).[34] If the agreement creates preferential treatment for US exporters to Japan, it violates MFN treatment for third country exporters. This was precisely the contention of the EC which took its complaint to GATT.[35] The facts of the matter remain unclear, although Clyde Prestowitz claims that a secret side letter to the agreement did commit Japan to securing a numerical target for US exports in the Japanese market.[36] More generally, bilateral market access negotiations are an invitation to preferential treatment and discrimination.

In Spring 1988, a GATT panel rejected the EC complaint that the agreement gave the United States preferential access to the Japanese market. It did, however, find that Japan's method of implementing the pact, by maintaining prices through production and output controls and accomplishing this through administrative guidance, was illegal.

The Korean insurance market provides another example of how market opening efforts, when undertaken unilaterally, are likely to lead to discriminatory trade. Prompted by two American insurance companies, the US government initiated a section 301 investigation of Korea's policy of prohibiting or restricting foreign firms from selling life insurance and other types of insurance in Korea.[37] The US government requested access for an equal premium share in a mandatory fire insurance pool for two US firms already established with branches in Korea, and entry by new US firms in both insurance markets (life insurance and other types of insurance) in Korea. The negotiated results (after a threat of retaliation directed against Korean exports to the United States) included access to the fire pool and its premiums by the two US firms, a commitment to licence one US firm in the life insurance market by the end of 1986, and a commitment to licence other qualified US firms in both insurance markets. The *de facto* result is not an MFN multilateral liberalization of trade in insurance services, but the licensing of US firms, obviously giving them preferential access over other foreign suppliers.

The US beef negotiations with Japan provide another example of how aggressive policy to improve access for US exports may increase discrimination in trade, even if this is not the intent. The 1984 US–Japan Beef Understanding and the subsequent agreement between Japan and Australia called for a 9,000 ton per year increase for four years in the Japanese global beef import quota. However, Japan agreed to increase the import of high quality beef, within the overall quota increase, by 6,900 tons per year. High quality beef is almost exclusively supplied by the United States, and thus the United States would receive 77 percent of the total quota increase, although its share in total Japanese beef imports was initially 28 percent.[38]

These examples show that cajoling or pressuring foreign governments into improving market access are likely to result in increased *de facto* discrimination, returning the United States to trade practices by and large abandoned by the end of the nineteenth century. More broadly, in the three areas examined – increased protection, preferential trade agreements and bilateral market access talks – there has been a decided tilt under President Reagan away from the principle of nondiscrimination.

Aggressive reciprocity and unfair trade practices

The traditional tools for dealing with so-called unfair trade practices have been antidumping and countervailing duty legislation and section 337 of the Tariff Act of 1930, the latter being used mainly to exclude goods that infringe patent or trademark law.[39] The president does not initiate these cases and has no direct role in the decisions, and thus in most instances their outcome offers little direct insight into presidential tilt on trade matters.[40]

Section 301 of the 1974 trade act offers clearer evidence of the administration's trade philosophy with regard to so-called unfair trade. First, section 301 cases are decided by the president and indeed can be initiated by him or by the USTR, as well as by petition from the private sector. Second, section 301 has become the principal tool of the new policy of aggressive reciprocity, and represents a significant departure in the conduct of US trade policy. These trade provisions, first included in the Trade Act of 1974, give the president very broad authority to attack foreign trade practices that are unilaterally determined by the United States to be "unreasonable, unjustifiable or discriminatory" and a burden to US commerce. Should negotiations with the foreign government over the removal of these practices fail, the president is authorized to retaliate, using a broad array of trade instruments and not limiting the retaliation to the particular sector or product at issue.

The ostensible reason for section 301 is not protectionist. It does, however, depart from the traditional tenets and conduct of liberal trade. First, it is a unilateral action by the United States and attempts to remove a foreign trade barrier without any equivalent concession by the United States. This violates the traditional notion of reciprocity as reciprocal concessions by governments that have voluntarily convened to liberalize trade. Second, section 301 can be used to attack practices that are not illegal under GATT rules or US trade agreements. The term "unjustifiable" implies violation of US rights, but "unreasonable" is defined to include any act, policy or practice that, while not necessarily in violation of US rights, is deemed to be unfair and inequitable. In turn, "unfair" and "inequitable" are defined to cover practices that deny to the United States market opportunities or opportunities to establish an enterprise, or that deny protection of intellectual property rights. The power to unilaterally declare a foreign trade practice unfair and to retaliate violates the liberal trade principle of adherence to internationally agreed-upon rules. Third, in contrast to the traditional notion of reciprocity, section 301 operates under the threat of retaliation (not unlike the penalty tariffs of earlier days). Obviously, it is a tool that can only be used by large countries with important markets. Fourth, as noted above, section 301 has the potential for discrimination by creating preferential access for US exports. Finally, the thrust of section 301 shades into demands that foreign governments afford access, on a product-by-product and country-by-country basis, that is equivalent to access offered by the United States, and that market access initiatives should be directed toward obtaining bilateral balances in trade, or at least a reduction in foreign bilateral trade surpluses.

The use of section 301 accelerated sharply after the administration, responding to political charges of neglecting trade, formed its trade policy strike force in 1985. Between September 7, 1985, and June 15, 1988, the United States challenged foreign practices 26 times by expediting, initiating or threatening to initiate section 301 investigations, with a considerable number initiated by the administration and not by petition from the private sector. Three of the cases resulted in retaliation.[41] Interestingly, in 1986 and again in 1988 the administration chose not to accept a private sector petition for a section 301 action to liberalize the Japanese rice market, despite that country's near total import ban on rice.

The use of section 301 has been supplemented by a number of direct efforts at improving US export access taken outside of any multilateral trade talks. The most important have been the Market-Oriented-Sector Specific (MOSS) Talks with Japan, covering telecommunications, medical equipment and pharmaceutical products, electronics, forest products and auto parts. Finally, the telecommunications provisions of the 1988 omnibus trade legislation call for equivalent foreign market access in this sector, and, like section 301, are a response to rising demand for reciprocity.

In summary, US trade policy has become more active, defending import-competing industries from fair and "unfair" competition, unilaterally graduating countries from the GSP, and aggressively attempting to open markets to US exports through bilateral talks. The actions by the administration were clearly in response to political pressures expressed forcefully in Congress. However, this response by the administration to domestic demands has created pressures on trading partners to accommodate the United States in ways that depart significantly from traditional trade liberalization and may have a chilling effect on trade. For example, without any explicit US trade restraint, South Korea is reportedly restricting exports of at least 18 products, including video tape recorders, microwave ovens, color televisions, pianos, and fishing rods, with a value of over $1.8 billion, in an effort to forestall protectionist action. These preemptive voluntary export restraints are the antithesis of liberal trade.[42]

Export subsidies

The Reagan administration's record with regard to export subsidies appears to be one of good intentions, but distressingly little progress. The administration attempted to cut back funding for the US Export–Import Bank in its first two annual budgets, but by 1983 was supporting a modest expansion of the lending authority.[43] In addition, the bank, which had traditionally provided subsidized loans and loan guarantees for five or more years, introduced medium-term (one- to five-year) lending. Additionally, becoming frustrated with extensive use of so-called "mixed credits" by European governments, in which small amounts of foreign aid grants are combined with commercial lending to lower overall financing costs, the United States proposed a $300 million Treasury Department fund to create its own mixed credit scheme. The first such package was used to subsidize telecommunications equipment exports to Gabon.[44]

The administration has also backed down in its initial distaste for agricultural export subsidies, and by October 1982 the Agriculture Department was offering export loans below commercial market rates in an attempt to match subsidized European exports. This was the first direct subsidy of US farm exports since 1972. Shortly after the initiation of direct subsidies, the Agriculture Department provided surplus wheat for sale at below world market prices to Egypt, an action bitterly protested by the EC, despite a similar sale by the EC a year earlier.[45] By and large, subsequent subsidies for agricultural exports have been used defensively, to counter European and other exporting country sales in traditional markets. In 1986 the administration agreed to subsidize wheat sales to the Soviet Union. The short-term policy has been to match European agricultural subsidies, but it must be acknowledged that the longer-term stated objective is to phase out agricultural export subsidies. In this regard, the United States has pushed strongly for ultimate elimination of agricultural export subsidies in the Uruguay Round.

The Domestic International Sales Corporation (DISC) Scheme was first initiated in 1971 as a tax incentive to encourage exporting. The heart of the DISC scheme is deferral of tax on export earnings. Taxes deferred represent an interest-free loan and hence can be considered a subsidy to exporters. The Carter administration attempted to repeal DISC legislation, but was unsuccessful. Moreover, a GATT panel had found the DISC scheme to be an illegal export subsidy. The response of the Reagan administration was not to attempt a repeal, but to find GATT-compatible legislation that would continue to offer tax advantages to US firms for exporting. Such a device was found, and a tax preference scheme for exports continues in a slightly modified form.

Trade policy as the handmaiden of foreign policy

An unbending commitment to *free* trade proscribes the use of trade policy to secure noncommercial foreign policy objectives. A commitment to *liberal* trade does not flatly reject such policies, but does demand sparing use.[46] Evaluating administration performance in this area is difficult because of the diversity of the economic instruments that are used, the diversity of foreign policy goals that are sought, and the considerable and direct role of Congress.

The objectives to which foreign economic policy tools are directed are also diverse – to maintain military security, to destabilize foreign regimes that are not supported by the United States, to punish or reward votes in the United Nations, to prevent nuclear proliferation, to control terrorism, or to improve human rights abroad. For these reasons conclusive evidence of the Reagan administration's willingness to use trade as a tool of foreign policy is difficult to establish.

Perhaps the most contentious issue *within* the Reagan administration with regard to the use of trade for noncommercial objectives was that of controls over the export of strategic goods and technology to the Eastern Bloc. The main protagonists were the Defense Department, which favored strict controls, and the Commerce Department, which wished to relax and to streamline export controls. Such a debate is not productive for understanding a commitment to liberal trade, however, as military security will take precedence over trade philosophy, and the debate will then turn on the type of export controls that are most likely to maximize security and minimize unnecessary restraint on exports.

A brief review of the Reagan administration's use of trade policy to secure noncommercial, nonmilitary objectives suggests that, although there had been a shift in emphasis in the objectives as compared with the Carter presidency, the overall use remained active. By and large, the Carter administration employed economic sanctions to improve human rights and to force adherence to nuclear safeguards. The human rights cases included economic sanctions against Uruguay, Ethiopia, Paraguay, Guatemala, Chile, Argentina, Nicaragua, El Salvador, the Soviet Union, and Brazil.[47] The instruments used were generally not direct trade controls, but reduction of economic assistance, curtailment of military sales, and pressure on multilateral institutions to reduce loans. According to summaries compiled by Hufbauer and Schott, many of these economic sanctions lapsed during the first three years of the Reagan administration, but sometimes for the valid reason that human rights conditions had indeed improved.

The Reagan administration has not hesitated to use economic sanctions to punish or destabilize foreign regimes to whose policies or existence it objects. Some examples are the following: economic sanctions against Nicaragua, including reallocation of Nicaragua's sugar quota to other Central American countries; revocation of MFN status and other economic sanctions against Poland; economic action against Argentina in support of the United Kingdom in the Falkland Islands crisis; suspension of aid, in coordination with the Netherlands, to Surinam to diminish Cuban and Soviet influence in that country; economic retaliation against the Soviet Union for shooting down a Korean commercial aircraft; and at one time or another the withholding of aid from Grenada, Haiti, the Philippines, Panama, and others.

The grain embargo against the Soviet Union and the oil pipeline dispute were perhaps the most controversial sanction cases in recent years. In January 1980 President Carter embargoed grain exports to the Soviet Union in retaliation for the invasion of Afghanistan. The embargo was unpopular domestically, and in April 1981 President Reagan lifted it on grounds that it proved ineffective in penalizing the Soviet Union. Subsequently, the United

UNIVERSITY OF BRISTOL LIBRARY
WITHDRAWN

States pledged to the Soviet Union not to use export controls for foreign policy purposes in the grain trade. Shortly thereafter, however, the administration placed an embargo on the sale of US equipment for building a gas pipeline from the Soviet Union to Western Europe, and extended the ban to foreign subsidiaries of US companies and to foreign companies producing under US license. This action was bitterly resented and defied by European governments, and the United States subsequently backed down. The grain embargo case suggests that the Reagan administration was concerned with the ineffectiveness of the sanctions as well as the harm done to US commercial interests, but that these same concerns did not initially prevail in the pipeline dispute.

Interpretation and conclusions

A limited view of *laissez-faire*

The preceding discussion makes quite clear that, whatever the rhetorical economic philosophy of the Reagan administration, a policy of free trade, as defined by an unbending commitment to deregulate import and export markets and to sever government involvement in trade, was never seriously pursued. The zeal that was applied to cutting taxes and reducing the role of government in the domestic economy did not motivate trade policy. At most there were sporadic efforts, some successful, some not, to resist new levels of protection, and to seek partial liberalization by launching the Uruguay Round and concluding a free trade agreement with Canada.

The failure to extend Reaganomics to the international sector by declaring free trade, unilaterally if necessary, is not altogether surprising.[48] Free trade has never been overly popular in the United States. Even in the heyday of liberal trade, the freeing of trade was always pursued and defended in mercantilist terms, especially in terms of improving access to foreign markets. Import liberalization in the United States, since 1934, has been conditioned on reciprocal liberalization by our trade partners. Even the GATT, which has been a principal forum for liberalization, is based on the mercantilist premise that a reduction in an import barrier is a "cost" or a "concession" and that reciprocity requires that cost to be compensated by an equivalent "benefit". One of the most powerful conclusions from economics – that with very limited exceptions, free trade is beneficial regardless of the behavior of trade partners – has been and remains an academic proposition. The doctrine of free trade has left policy makers and the public unmoved and unconvinced. Seen in this context, the failure of the Reagan administration to extend its commitment to *laissez-faire* to international trade is understandable, but it is perhaps regrettable.

To dismiss the possibility of free trade as outside US traditions and beyond political realism, is to severely limit the scope of Reagan's economic philosophy. Despite the commitment of the administration to private enterprise and the magic of the marketplace, there was no recognition that the philosophy logically extends to international markets. Through a curious blind spot, those who would roll back government involvement in the domestic economy did precious little to roll back the interventionist role of the US government in international markets.[49]

Why there was a failure to extend the Reagan economic program to the area of trade remains unclear. One of the strongest advocates of free trade within the administration, William Niskanen, describes trade policy under Reagan as a strategic retreat, and suggests that at least initially it was simply considered unimportant.[50] Key appointments may not have helped. Malcolm Baldrige, Secretary of Commerce, certainly did not carry the ball for free trade, and William Brock, as Trade Representative, was known as an able negotiator, but not for his passion for free trade. A powerful advocate of free trade, at the highest level, was missing.

Assessment

If a free trade policy was never contemplated, how is the record on liberal trade to be assessed? A defense of the Reagan administration's performance in maintaining and promoting liberal trade might run along these lines. First, the domestic and international circumstances were increasingly hostile to liberal trade. These circumstances included a massive trade deficit, a longer-term erosion of support for liberal trade among the traditional constituencies within the United States, and a declining hegemonic position of the United States in the world economy. Second, given this difficult context, the record is not bad at all. The Uruguay Round of trade negotiations has been launched, a free trade agreement with Canada has been negotiated, representing a regional stepping stone toward freer trade, and Congress, which has yet to pass a veto-proof, outright protectionist trade bill, has been held in check.

Third, one could argue that the basic assumptions of the free trade model no longer obtain. Comparative advantage is increasingly the contrived and artificial result of governments intervening in the economy. Moreover, much of world production is characterized by imperfect competition and increasing returns to scale. Recent theoretical work suggests that in such situations government involvement via import restrictions and export subsidies *may* be in the national interest.[51] Hence it could be argued that government intervention in trade during the Reagan administration, while departing from *laissez-faire*, responded precisely to the types of market failures that even the most conservative economic philosophy could accept as requiring government action.

On the first argument, it is of course true that the US merchandise trade deficit grew to unprecedented proportions, from $28 billion in 1981 to $122 billion in 1985 and $160 billion in 1987. And there is no question that a deficit of this magnitude puts enormous strain on the US tradeable goods sector, increases demand for protection and export assistance, and makes defense of liberal trade principles exceedingly difficult.[52]

But the trade deficit is a lame excuse for whatever backsliding took place, for the deficit itself is generally considered to be the result of the administration's macroeconomic policies, and especially fiscal policy.[53] In turn, there is general, if not universal, agreement among economists that the strength of the dollar through March 1985 was related to the extraordinary tax cuts of 1981, which raised after-tax returns on financial assets and which, coupled with heavy defense spending, created massive federal deficits. With declining personal savings and large government dissaving by virtue of the federal budget deficit, domestic expenditure exceeded output, national savings fell short of investment and the trade deficit ballooned. In short, Reagan's fiscal policy of tax cuts and defense spending were a major contributing factor to the trade deficit and thus contributed directly to protectionist pressure.

By and large, in its first term the administration did not acknowledge any threat to liberal trade arising from the dollar and the macroeconomic policy mix. It was not until 1985, with the move of James Baker from the White House to his position as Secretary of the Treasury, that the administration developed an active strategy to counter protection. Curiously, the two prongs of that policy were a concerted international effort to accelerate the then declining value of the dollar by central bank intervention, thus reversing the *laissez-faire* exchange rate policy of the previous four years, and the creation of a trade policy strike force directed at foreign trade barriers, fair and unfair.[54] There was no action directed against the proximate arithmetic "cause" of the trade deficit, i.e. domestic expenditure in excess of output, and tax increases continued to be ruled out. Equally significant, in the Tax Reform Act of 1986, the most massive tax overhaul in a generation, virtually no attention was paid to the effect of the act on savings and investment, and hence the macroeconomic imbalance that had been building since 1981. We may conclude, therefore, that the main lines of macroeconomic policy during the Reagan administration directly if unintentionally contributed to a domestic political and economic environment hostile to liberal trade.

The trade deficit, however, tells only part of the antiliberal or protectionist story. Well before the advent of the Reagan administration, domestic and international forces were working to undermine the liberal character of postwar US trade policy, and the continuation of these forces set the context for Reagan's trade policy.

The most sweeping explanation, discussed by Baldwin in this volume, is that the liberal trade policy of the United States in the early postwar period was an artifact of the hegemonic position of the United States in the world economy, and that those days are gone. A liberal trade system is said to have elements of a public good, especially if viewed in mercantilistic terms where market access is thought to be of greater importance than inexpensive imports. In the earlier postwar period, the United States was prepared to provide the public good – basically to extend greater trade concessions than it received and to tolerate the discriminatory character of the European Economic Community – for political reasons and because the dominant economic position of the United States guaranteed adequate and sometimes exceptional export markets.[55]

According to this explanation conditions have changed radically. The perceived costs of unilaterally maintaining a liberal trade system have increased and our willingness to do so has decreased. We are retreating to a more nationalistic commercial policy, albeit not one based on the small country gains from free trade, but based on our older traditions of mercantilism.

Thus it can be argued that the Reagan administration was confronted with a trade environment that was no longer congruent with the liberal trade system which the United States had championed in the early postwar period. While the administration certainly did not seek to scrap the entire system, it has attempted to reshape it significantly in directions that serve narrower national and commercial interests, whether or not they promote the classic liberal trade system.

The final argument in defense of its performance is that the Reagan administration cleverly recognized that a strategic trade policy, involving selective but active government involvement in trade, was needed to deal with market imperfections and economies of scale, and was therefore in the national interest. There may be a kernel of truth here, but the argument is not totally persuasive, nor is there much evidence that, had this been the rationale for an interventionist trade policy, it has been notably successful. One reason for being skeptical is that even strategic trade theorists acknowledge that theoretical and empirical difficulties, and elementary propositions from political economy, make the implementation of a rational strategic trade policy exceptionally difficult. For these reasons they strongly caution against departures from free trade.[56] And from the other side, even the proponents of a strategic trade policy within the administration bemoan the inaction of the government in recent years, suggesting that strategic considerations played little or no role in policy.[57]

A second reason for doubting whether trade policy was grounded in the new strategic trade theory is the nature of the interventions themselves. In many, though not all, of the industries receiving additional protection under the Reagan administration (for example, sugar, textiles and garments, heavy-duty motorcycles, and canned mushrooms), the prerequisites for the new theory, which are increasing returns to scale and technological externalities, are implausible. The same is true for many, although not all, US export products promoted through section 301 actions, such as almonds in India, tobacco sales in Korea and Japan (external diseconomics!), and EC exports of pasta to third country markets. These are not the sorts of products from which economies of scale or technological spin-off advantages can be derived.

In some other sectors, however, strategic trade concerns may have played a role, as for example the semiconductor dispute with Japan, the dispute over the Brazilian informatics policy which restricts computers and software imports, and the dispute with the European Community over subsidized sales of the Airbus. Whether these are examples of effective and rational strategic trade policy is another question. On balance, it appears that the effectiveness of domestic interest groups and the effectiveness of domestic and international politics have been the principal factors determining which sectors would benefit from active administration involvement in trade, but that concerns related to technological externalities were not totally absent.

The myth of fair and unfair trade

Perhaps the most striking feature of the debate over trade policy in the past eight years is the emergence of the doctrine of fair trade as the touchstone of US trade policy. It is true that throughout the history of US commercial policy, the call for "fair trade" has been seductive, underlying the pauper labor arguments for protection, the earlier insistence on conditional MFN status, and the search for the "scientific tariff" early in this century. But the shrillness and persistence of demands for fair trade, and the conviction that virtually all other countries practice unfair trade, crippling a fair-trading United States, are of recent origin.[58]

It is hard to say how this view has gained such currency and widespread acceptance. Perhaps the constant drumbeat of the assertion has made it a revealed truth. Until 1980, the proposition that the world was unfair and the United States fair remained an assertion; by 1988 it had become accepted as a fact, beyond question, among most policy makers and with the general public. More importantly, it had become the cornerstone of US trade policy and a principal excuse for poor US trade performance.

This is a curious development. There is little evidence that the *level* of explicit foreign trade barriers among industrial countries is higher than in the United States.[59] It is true that the general level of import barriers in developing countries is higher than in the United States, but there is no evidence that these barriers have increased in recent years or that these countries systematically discriminate against the United States. Indeed, several important developing countries are unilaterally dismantling trade barriers. And, in any event, US import restrictions are disproportionally directed against these countries. Even if the general level of trade barriers is higher abroad, this level surely has not increased substantially over the past eight years, and can in no way account for the increase in the US trade deficit of $130 billion during this period.

In short, the fixation on unfair trade looks like a convenient excuse for a poor trade performance that has its roots in recent US macroeconomic policy, and, more speculatively, in a fundamental long-term decline in the international competitive position of the United States. It would be a mistake, however, to quantify and dismiss the appeal of the unfair trade and the unlevel playing field arguments by simply counting the number of changes in explicit US and foreign import barriers. In point of fact, the charge of unfair trade practices is much broader, if not precisely defined.

This new view of unfair trade argues that foreign governments systematically, purposefully, and pervasively intervene in their economies to gain international commercial advantage. The list of practices is too long to enumerate, ranging from covert credit allocation to the tolerance of export cartels, and from sly use of product standards for covert protection to stalling tactics with the GATT. The principal "culprits" in this view are Japan, the newly industrializing countries (NICs), and from time to time the European Community. The tolerance in the United States for "artificial" comparative advantage, derived from systematic government intervention, has become thin indeed.

This new view of the world as fundamentally unfair did not originate with the Reagan administration, but it is fair to say that that administration embraced it when it suited domestic political needs. In this regard, the excessive emphasis on Japan as the root source of US trade difficulties and the near obsession with disciplining Japanese import and export policies comes to mind, as does the active use of section 301 in a highly visible response to domestic political challenges.[60] In this regard, the Reagan trade policy, at least since 1985, has paid more attention to domestic politics than international economics. The domestic political results, however, are modest. A retail approach to identifying and challenging foreign unfair trade practices, product by product, country by country, and replete with negotiated compromises, has failed to impress Congress, while lending credibility to the thesis that foreigners play unfair and that the solution to US trade problems rests with even more vigorous assertion of US "rights."

To its credit, the Reagan administration did not panic in responding to the myth of unfair trade, especially the alleged advantage gained by foreigners from "industrial policy." Consistent with its economic philosophy, the

Reagan administration did not support a *general* domestic policy in the United States aimed at targeting so-called sunrise industries with cheap credit, favorable tax treatment, or other favors. Nor did it pursue a consistent and planned policy of protection *cum* export subsidies to those industries, much to the regret of those who would challenge the Japanese by policy imitation. When pressed by domestic politics, however, it did not hesitate to push the fair trade theme. In short, it did little to dispel the myth of unfair trade, and in some respects has lent it undeserved credibility.

Legacy and outlook

The net result of the past eight years is a trade policy that is in considerable disarray. The Reagan administration made no attempt to initiate an era of free trade. Indeed it was never seriously contemplated. The defense of liberal trade gains over the past three decades was weak and not particularly effective. The initiative for trade policy has slipped over to a frustrated Congress. The root causes of the US trade problem, the macroeconomics imbalances resulting in excessive US expenditures, and perhaps more fundamental reasons for declining international competitiveness, were not addressed. If one credits the declining hegemony argument, the response of the United States has not been to seek out the gains from free trade available to a small country, but to use its remaining economic power to push its immediate commercial interests without great regard for preserving the traditional principles of liberal trade. The elevation of US commercial interests is new in postwar US policy. It signals a willingness to risk cooperative relations in a wide range of foreign policy areas to secure market access and to stamp out whatever the United States determines to be an unfair trade practice.

An evaluation of the two major trade-liberalizing initiatives, the US–Canada Free-Trade Agreement and the Uruguay Round, remains premature. The first is an historic departure from US trade principles that weakens the GATT system of multilateralism and nondiscrimination, but may in the end be a necessary and successful detour toward freer trade. The outcome of the second initiative is even more speculative with the inclusion of new and problematic issues involving (certain) services, intellectual property, and trade-related investment issues. The first two Uruguay Round issues follow the long US tradition of seeking commercial advantage in areas of purported comparative advantage, and reflect the need to patch together a new domestic constituency for liberal trade. A framework for agreements in these areas might strengthen a liberal trade order, especially if based on the principle of nondiscrimination and national treatment. But the attempt to extend GATT to new areas when it is manifestly frail in its traditional functions is risky.

The Bush administration confronts considerable difficulties in trade policy. The trade deficit, while showing signs of improvement, is likely to persist for some time. The recent backsliding in liberal trade policy will be difficult to reverse. Domestic interest groups have had major success in receiving protection over the past eight years, and will press for more. It is unlikely that the new administration will embrace an even more extreme *laissez-faire* economic philosophy, and therefore will not have available this shield against protectionist pressure. Congress has tasted new power in trade – actually, regaining some of its original powers – and will demand a major role. The partial reversion to the trade policy characteristic of the United States in the nineteenth century and the strong underlying mercantilist traditions within the country will further limit a new administration. Foreign resistance to US dicta on what is unfair trade is likely to increase.

Perhaps most importantly, the new gospel of fair trade and the Reagan administration's response of aggressive reciprocity, which has been supported and encouraged by Congress, will limit and shape trade policy. The conviction that foreigners are fundamentally unfair and that it is the right and responsibility of the US government to make over foreign economic policies to give us some commercial advantage, and to do this on a unilateral basis using the threat of trade retaliation, is the major change of the 1980s. "Fairness" in trade is inherently subjective. Other countries are unlikely in the extreme to welcome and quietly accept our standards of fairness. The greater unfairness, from their perspective, may be unilateral pressures from the United States backed by the threat of retaliation. The economic power of the United States may be waning, but it can still disrupt the trade system. It will be a major challenge to accommodate the domestic demands for "fair trade" without retreating to greater protection and while making sparing use of aggressive reciprocity.

Notes

* A longer version of this paper was published by the Johns Hopkins Foreign Policy Institute in 1989.

1 By 1807 re-exports accounted for 56 percent of total US exports, reaching a value of $60 million. Harold Underwood Faulkner, Harry N. Schreiber, and Harold G. Vatter, *American Economic History* (New York: Harper and Row, 1976), p. 116.

2 The Embargo Act prohibited any vessel to sail from the United States to any foreign port; the Non-Intercourse Act relaxed this extreme measure by only prohibiting trade with France and Great Britain. Chester Whitney Wright, *Economic History of the United States* (New York: McGraw-Hill, 1949), p. 205.

3 Cited by F. W. Taussig, *The Tariff History of the United States* (New York: G. P. Putnam Sons, 1931), p. 363.

4 In the 1820s the duty on wool was raised to 30 percent and woolen manufacturers complained that although they were as efficient as English producers, the high price of wool put them at a competitive disadvantage. Ibid., p. 43.

5 Ibid., p. 405.

6 Compare President Taft's determination with United States Trade Representative's *Foreign Trade Barriers* report for 1987 which runs to 338 pages.

7 See James Riedel, "United States Trade Policy: From Multilateralism to Bilateralism?" in *Toward Free World Trade*, Herbert Giersch, ed. (Tubingen: J. C. B. Mohr, 1987), pp. 85–104.

8 The 1854 Treaty was abrogated by the United States after ten years. A new attempt was made in 1911 and passed by Congress, but was rejected by the Canadian Parliament in large measure on nationalistic grounds.

9 The instruments for improving market access included so-called bargaining tariffs (both penalty tariffs and concessionary tariffs).

10 Benjamin H. Williams, *Economic Foreign Policy of the United States* (New York: Howard Fertig, 1967), p. 257.

11 Jagdish N. Bhagwati and Douglas A. Irwin, "The Return of the Reciprocitarians – U.S. Trade Policy Today," *World Economy*, 10(2) (June 1987): 109–31.

12 See William R. Cline, *"Reciprocity": A New Approach to World Trade Policy?* (Washington, DC: Institute for International Economics, 1982); and R. J. Wannacott, *Aggressive U.S. Reciprocity* (Montreal: The Institute for Research on Public Policy, 1984). One could argue of course that US and European efforts to secure trade privileges in China in the nineteenth century and Commodore Perry's mission to Japan in 1853 were forceful examples of an earlier policy of aggressive reciprocity.

13 There were some 30 reciprocity bills introduced in the 97th Congress. Cline, *Reciprocity*, p. 97.

14 Robert E. Baldwin, *The Political Economy of U.S. Import Policy* (Cambridge, Massachusetts: MIT Press, 1985), p. 34.

15 J. J. Pincus, "Why Have U.S. Tariffs Fallen Since 1930?" in *Issues in World Trade Policy*, R. H. Snape, ed. (New York: St. Martins Press, 1986), p. 238.

16 The term "substantial cause" is interpreted as a cause that is both "important" and no less important than any other single cause.

17 William A. Niskanen, *Reaganomics: An Insider's Account of the Policies and the People* (New York: Oxford University Press, 1988), p. 139.

18 According to Evans and Novak, the advocates of auto restrictions included Transportation Secretary Drew Lewis, Commerce Secretary Malcolm Baldrige and Labor Secretary Raymond Donovan. Opponents included Donald Regan, David Stockman, and Murray Weidenbaum, Chairman of the Council of Economic Advisors. Special Trade Representative William Brock negotiated the agreement. Rowland Evans and Robert Novak, *The Reagan Revolution* (New York: E. P. Dutton, 1981), p. 153.

19 William R. Cline, *The Future of World Trade in Textiles and Apparel* (Washington, DC: Institute for International Economics, 1987), p. 155.

20 I. M. Destler and John S. Odell, *Anti-Protection: Changing Forces in United States Trade Politics* (Washington, DC: Institute for International Economics, 1987), p. 16.
21 Cline, *The Future of World Trade*, pp. 213–20.
22 Destler and Odell, *Anti-Protection*, p. 14.
23 Gary Clyde Hufbauer, Diane T. Berliner, and Kimberly Ann Elliot, *Trade Protection in the United States: 31 Cases* (Washington, DC: Institute for International Economics, 1985), p. 284.
24 Prestowitz, Clyde W., *Trading Places: How We Allowed Japan to Take the Lead* (New York: Basic Books, 1988), pp. 227–9.
25 US Department of Commerce, International Trade Administration, "Fact Sheet: Machine Tools," *News* (Washington, DC: US Department of Commerce, undated).
26 Above a 5.6 percent average tariff (1983). Morris E. Morkre and David G. Tarr, *Aggregate Costs to the United States of Tariffs and Quotas on Imports* (Washington, DC: Federal Trade Commission, 1984), p. 126.
27 Ibid.
28 This protection is in addition to the protection granted specialty (stainless) to steel in 1983 and extended in 1987.
29 Charles F. Doran and Timothy J. Naftali, *U.S.–Canadian Softwood Lumber: Trade Dispute Negotiations* (Washington, DC: Johns Hopkins Foreign Policy Institute, 1987).
30 Ibid., p. 14.
31 "Copper Import Relief Decision," *Federal Register*, 49(177), 11 September, 1984.
32 Paul Wannacott, "The Canadian–U.S. Free Trade Agreement and the Auto Pact," *Trade Monitor* (C. D. Howe Institute, March 1988).
33 US conversion to unconditional MFN was not absolute. "Contingent duties" are to be found in the tariff acts of 1922 and 1930. Viner, Jacob (1951) *International Economics* (Glencoe, Ill.), p. 104.
34 Bhagwati and Irwin, "The Return of the Reciprocitarians," p. 126. VIEs are, of course, no more voluntary than are voluntary export restraints.
35 James W. Prendergast, "The European Economic Community's Challenge to the U.S.–Japan Semiconductor Arrangement," *Law and Policy in International Business*, 19(3) (1987): 579–603.
36 Prestowitz, *Trading Places*, p. 65.
37 For details, see Cho Yoon-Je, "How the United States Broke into Korea's Insurance Market" *World Economy*, 10(4) (December 1987): 483–96.
38 William T. Coyle, "The U.S.–Japan Beef and Citrus Understanding: An Evaluation," *Foreign Agricultural Economic Report*, no. 222 (US Department of Agriculture, July 1986), p. 1.
39 US antidumping legislation can be traced back to 1916, and countervailing duty legislation back to 1897.
40 There are important exceptions. For example, in 1982 Secretary of Commerce Baldrige negotiated steel quotas with the EC in return for which US steel producers dropped pending antidumping and countervailing duty cases. Another example is Canadian softwood lumber, originally a countervailing duty case,

which was ultimately resolved by a USTR negotiated agreement reached after President Reagan himself publicly promised to resolve the issue.

41 Office of the United States Trade Representative, "The President's Trade Policy: An Update" (Washington, DC: mimeo, 15 June 1988).

42 Charles S. Pearson, "United States–Korean Relations: The Economic Dimension," paper prepared for joint SAIS/IFANS Conference on Northeast Asia, Seoul, 14–16 December 1987, p. 13.

43 *Congressional Quarterly*, 19 February 1983, p. 375.

44 Bureau of National Affairs, *International Trade Reporter*, 3(22) (28 May 1986): 709.

45 *Congressional Quarterly*, 19 February 1983, p. 380.

46 Hufbauer et al. note that enthusiasm for economic sanctions goes through cycles. Gary Clyde Hufbauer, Jeffrey J. Schott and Kimberly Ann Elliot, *Economic Sanctions Reconsidered: History and Current Policy* (Washington, DC: Institute for International Economics, 1985) p. 8.

47 Ibid.

48 Edmund Dell correctly states "The doctrine of free trade dictates free access to foreign products *irrespective* of what other countries may do." Edmund Dell, "Of Free Trade and Reciprocity," *World Economy*, 9(2) (June 1986): 126.

49 An alternative explanation might be that the Reagan administration has been guided, not by principle, but by a pro-business pragmatism, which translates into reducing onerous requirements on business domestically, protecting US business from import competition, and promoting US business abroad.

50 Niskanen, *Reaganomics*, 137. "The implicit assumption was that international conditions were not an important consideration affecting policy."

51 For its policy implications, see Paul Krugman, "Is Free Trade Passé?" *Journal of Economic Perspectives*, 1(2) (Fall 1987): 131.

52 Takacs shows that the state of the economy and the trade balance are determinants of the pressure for protection, but not whether protection was granted. Wendy Takacs, "Pressures for Protection: An Empirical Analysis," *Economic Inquiry*, 19 (October 1981): 687.

53 For example, the 1985 Council of Economic Advisors Report to the President concludes that perhaps 25 percent of the deterioration in trade was due to income growth differentials and a large part of the remaining 75 percent was due to the strong dollar.

54 It remains an open question whether the Plaza agreement of September 1985 did little more than alter the time profile of the fall of the dollar, which had started to drop in March. Since then the United States has attempted not only to actively manage the overall value of its dollar, but has tried to manipulate the pattern of bilateral rates, including using the threat of trade retaliation against countries that in US judgement have failed to appreciate sufficiently.

55 US commitment was not 100 percent. The peril point provisions of the trade law provided some protection should liberalization lead to import competition that was too intense.

56 Krugman, "Is Free Trade Passé?"

57 Prestowitz, *Trading Places*.

58 It is significant that the Trade Act of 1984 calls for an annual report by USTR on foreign barriers to and distortions of trade, to include barriers affecting goods, services, investment, and intellectual property rights, whether or not such barriers are consistent or inconsistent with international trade rules. The latest report covers 40 countries and runs to 338 pages. There is no mention of US trade barriers.

59 For comparison of overt protection between the U.S. and Japan, see Fred C. Bergsten and William R. Cline, *The United States–Japan Economic Problem* (Washington, DC: Institute for International Economics, 1985).

60 In fact the US trade balance with Japan fell by $33 billion between 1980 and 1985, but fell by $44 billion with Western Europe over the same period.

3

US Trade Policy Toward Developing Countries

*Bela Balassa**

A policy adviser to developing countries, who recommends greater outward orientation for these countries, often encounters the reply that protectionism in the industrial world in general, and in the United States in particular, thwarts the efforts of countries that attempt to open their economies. The criticisms tend to be concentrated on the United States, which has the largest domestic market and whose actions have attracted the greatest publicity.

This chapter reviews the measures applied by the United States in regard to its imports from the developing countries, as well as actual changes in these imports. In the course of the discussion, comparisons with other major industrial countries, the European Community, and Japan, are also made.

1 Nontariff barriers to imports

As is well-known, industrial country tariffs have been greatly reduced in the course of multilateral trade negotiations undertaken since the Second World War. Tariff reductions have been extended to imports from the developing countries under the most-favored-nation clause, even though these countries have offered few concessions of their own.

While the lack of reciprocal concessions has meant that tariffs have been lowered less on products of interest to the developing countries than overall, the reductions have been very substantial. Thus, post-Tokyo Round import duties on semimanufactures and finished manufactures originating in the developing countries average only 8.7 percent in the United States, 6.7 percent in the European Community, and 6.8 percent in Japan.[1] Furthermore, within certain limits and excluding so-called sensitive items, duty-free entry has been provided for imports from the developing countries under the General Scheme of Preferences.

Table 3.1 Relative shares of imports from the developing countries subject to nontariff measures, 1985[a]

	US	*EEC*	*Japan*
All nonfuel products	12.9	21.8	10.5
Agricultural products	11.8	27.5	30.2
Manufactured products	14.4	21.4	5.4
Textiles and clothing	65.3	65.2	14.2
Footwear	0.0	12.5	42.2
Iron and Steel	4.5	28.9	0.0
Electrical machinery	0.0	4.7	0.0
Transport equipment	0.0	4.6	0.0
Other manufactures	1.9	5.3	1.9

[a] Figures calculated using world trade weights, and given as percentages of all imports from developing countries in the respective categories of imports.
Source: Nogues, Olechowski, and Winters, 1986, and the sources cited therein.

It has been charged, however, that reductions in tariffs have been more than offset by the increased application of nontariff measures that limit imports in quantitative terms. Among these measures, quantitative import restrictions, including import prohibitions, quotas, and import licensing, as well as so-called voluntary export restraints, limit imports directly. In turn, variable import levies, minimum price requirements for imports, "voluntary" export price restraints, and tariff quotas, involving the imposition of higher duties above a predetermined import quantity, have an indirect effect on imports.

Table 3.1 provides information on shares of imports subject to nontariff measures, calculated by using world trade weights. The use of world trade weights allows for differences in the relative importance of individual tariff items in international trade while abstracting from the idiosyncracies of national protection.[2] In contrast, calculating for a particular country the percentage share of imports subject to restrictions is equivalent to using the country's own imports as weights, which means that the more restrictive the measure the lower its weight in the calculations; in the extreme, prohibitive restrictions have zero weight.[3]

Table 3.1 gives figures for all nonfuel imports and, within this total, for agricultural and for manufactured imports in the United States, the European Community and Japan; it further disaggregates manufactured goods into textiles and clothing, footwear, iron and steel, electrical machinery, transport equipment, and other manufactures. Fuels have not been included because the nontariff measures applied do not appear to aim at protecting the domestic production of competing products, such as coal.

The data show that the United States applies nontariff measures to a smaller proportion of its agricultural imports originating in the developing countries than does either the European Community or Japan. This result reflects the fact that while the United States protects its sugar growers from imports originating in the developing countries, in the European Community and Japan protection extends to much of temperate zone agriculture.

The scope of manufactured imports from the developing countries that are subject to nontariff measures is also smaller in the United States than in the European Community. This is so for all product categories other than textiles and clothing, the imports of which are limited under the Multifiber Arrangement (MFA) in both cases. Thus, in contrast to the European Community, the United States does not employ nontariff measures to limit the imports of footwear, electrical machinery, and transport equipment from the developing countries. And, the share of commodities subject to such barriers is lower in the United States than in the European Community in the case of iron and steel as well as for other manufactures.

The reported share of manufactured goods, imported from developing countries, that are subject to nontariff measures is lower in Japan than in the United States. This is because Japan does not limit its textiles and clothing imports in the framework of the MFA and, apart from footwear, it has few formal restrictions on manufactured imports in the remaining categories. But Japan has imposed limitations on textiles and clothing imported from developing countries whenever such imports have assumed importance and has used informal measures of protection in regard to various other manufactured goods (Balassa, 1986a). The effects of these measures will be apparent as we consider the growth of imports from developing countries in section 3 below.

2 Other border measures

The data reported in table 3.1 do not include other border measures that can be, but are not always, used with protective intent. Countervailing actions, taken in response to export subsidies, and antidumping actions, taken in response to sales below cost or below the home-market price, as well as the initiation of investigations into such unfair trading practices and the monitoring of imports, have been placed in this category (Nogues, Olechowski, and Winters, 1986).[4]

Some authors have included countervailing and antidumping actions, investigations into unfair practices, and the monitoring of imports with the nontariff barriers described in section 1, and report data by combining the two sets of measures (Nogues, Olechowski, and Winters, 1986).[5] To evaluate this practice, the countervailing actions initiated in the United States will now be examined.

As shown in table 3.2, in the first half of the 1980s, substantial increases occurred in the United States in the number of petitions for countervailing action against developing country exporters. There were 112 such cases from 1980 to 1985, compared with two cases from 1973 to 1974 and 45 from 1975 to 1979. By contrast, the numbers of cases in the European Community and Japan were only three and one respectively in the 1980–5 period (Nam, 1986, tables 2 and 3).

While the number of countervailing actions against developing countries increased in the United States, the number of such actions against industrial countries declined compared with the 1975–9 period (table 3.2). This divergence may be explained by the fact that the Tokyo Round code on subsidies reaffirmed the prohibition of export subsidies by the industrial countries while for developing countries it maintained the possibility of granting export subsidies. Also, the large majority of countervailing actions were initiated against highly-indebted Latin American countries that instituted export subsidies during the periods under consideration,[6] and the share of affirmative decisions was generally greater and the countervailing duty rates substantially higher for these countries than for countries in the Far East.[7]

At the same time, an increasing number of petitions for countervailing action initiated in the United States against developing countries were settled by alternative arrangements, which did not involve the application of countervailing duties. In particular, the exporter's government might remove the subsidies that had given rise to the petition in the first place.

In turn, the share of negative decisions in the total declined by nearly one-half from the 1975–9 period to the 1980–5 period. All in all, the share of affirmative decisions in countervailing actions initiated against developing countries remained approximately the same, amounting to two-fifths of the total. But affirmative decisions accounted for only 1.5 percent of US imports from these countries in 1980–5, and the average countervailing duty levied was 13.2 percent. Thus, the additional duty imposed was less than 0.2 percent of US imports from the developing countries.

The number of countervailing duty cases against developing countries has declined to a considerable extent in recent years. Countervailing action was initiated in 20 cases in 1986, compared with 30 cases in 1984 and 28 in 1985. Moreover, there were only 6 cases of countervailing action initiated against developing countries in 1987.

The time pattern of countervailing duty cases may be explained by changes

Table 3.2 Countervailing actions in the United States against industrial and developing country exporters, 1970–87

			Final outcome				
Year(s)	*Exporting countries*	*Number of initiations*	*Affirmative*	*Alternative arrangements*[a]	*Negative*[b]	*Pending*	*Average countervailing duty rate*[c]
1970–4	Industrial	9	8	0	1	0	NA
	Developing	2	2	0	0	0	NA
1975–9	Industrial	59	20	0	39	0	NA
	Developing	45	18	0	27	0	NA
1980	Industrial	2	0	0	2	0	0
	Developing	6	5	1	0	0	8.3
1981	Industrial	6	0	1	5	0	0
	Developing	4	1	1	2	0	15.8
1982	Industrial	30	3	16	11	0	11.5
	Developing	31	13	13	5	0	10.2

1983	Industrial	3	2	0	1	0	10.7
	Developing	13	7	1	5	0	10.9
1984	Industrial	10	4	1	5	0	8.6
	Developing	30	11	7	12	0	12.7
1985	Industrial	12	5	2	5	0	15.5
	Developing	28	10	4	14	0	21.5
1986	Industrial	8	4	1	3	0	4.8
	Developing	20	12	2	6	0	37.8
1987	Industrial	3	1	0	2	0	25.1
	Developing	6	2	0	1	3	32.8
1980–7	Industrial	74	19	21	34	0	11.3
	Developing	138	61	29	45	3	18.4

[a] Cases withdrawn under an alternative arrangement involving e.g. the elimination of subsidies.
[b] Cases withdrawn voluntarily by petitioners or rejected by the authorities.
[c] Simple average of subsidy rates for affirmative cases. NA, not applicable.
Source: Table prepared by Ms Azita Amjadi of the World Bank.

in the value of the US dollar. Thus, the increased number of countervailing duty petitions after 1980 may find their origin in the growing overvaluation of the US dollar that accentuated the injury due to export subsidies. In turn, the subsequent depreciation of the dollar may have contributed to the observed decline in the number of countervailing duty cases by offsetting the injury due to export subsidization.

Between 1980 and 1985, the dollar appreciated by 29 percent in real terms, calculated by adjusting the trade-weighted average of the nominal exchange rate for changes in wholesale prices in the United States and abroad; the extent of appreciation was more than double the average rate of countervailing duties applied during this period. In turn, the dollar depreciated by 35 percent in real terms between 1985 and 1987.

At the same time, countervailing actions are "GATT-conforming" as they are sanctioned by Article VI of the General Agreement and they correct distortions due to export subsidies. And while it has been argued that the negative correlation between comparative advantage and countervailing and antidumping actions reflects a bias toward protectionism (Finger, Hall, and Nelson, 1982), it stands to reason that industries suffering from foreign competition will initiate such actions. This will be the case, in particular, when the injury test is applied, since industries that are at a comparative disadvantage are likely to suffer an injury as a result of export subsidization abroad.

It should further be noted that countervailing and antidumping actions involve the imposition of duties and are thus different in character from nontariff measures that limit imports in quantitative terms. One may also query the inclusion of investigations of unfair trading practices and the monitoring of imports under nontariff measures. While uncertainty is thereby created, this does not represent the actual application of nontariff measures.[8] Thus, it is appropriate to limit the scope of nontariff measures to the actions included in table 3.1.

3 Nontariff protection and imports

The next question concerns the protective effects of nontariff measures. For this purpose, the tariff equivalent of such measures may be calculated. Under competitive conditions, this can be expressed as the percentage difference between domestic and international prices, or the nominal rate of protection.

Nominal rates of protection have been estimated for agricultural products. While the averages have been calculated for a group of products of varying importance for the developing countries, the data indicate the overall level of agricultural protection in the industrial countries as well as changes over time.

Whereas average agricultural protection in the United States remained approximately nil, the extent of protection was high to begin with and subsequently increased further in the European Community and, in particular, in Japan during the 1960–80 period. Thus, the average nominal rate of protection for agricultural products rose from 41.1 percent in 1960 to 83.5 percent in Japan and from 32.8 percent to 35.7 percent in the European Community (Honma and Hayami, 1986). Utilizing data on nominal rates of protection and on supply and demand elasticities, it has further been estimated that, in terms of 1984 prices, the elimination of nontariff measures on agricultural products would lead to increases in imports of $8.8 billion in Japan, $12.4 billion in the European Community and $0.5 billion in the United States (Tyers and Anderson, 1986).

Price comparisons are difficult to make for most manufactured goods, which are largely differentiated products that vary in quality and specifications. In the absence of price comparisons, then, one cannot appropriately gauge the level of protection that nontariff measures on manufactured products provide.[9] However, the restrictiveness of nontariff measures may be indicated in an indirect way. For this purpose, use has been made of data on the share of imports from developing countries in the domestic consumption of manufactured goods in the industrial countries (the import penetration ratio). Table 3.3 provides this information for the United States, the European Community, and Japan, for the years 1973, 1978, 1983, 1985, and 1987.

The data show that, during the period under consideration, the import-penetration ratio for manufactured goods increased the most in the United States, followed by the European Community and, much behind, Japan. Thus, while the ratio rose from 1.1 percent in 1973 to 4.6 percent in 1987 in the United States, the increases were from 0.9 to 2.7 percent in the European Community and from 0.7 to 1.3 percent in Japan.

Table 3.3 Relative importance of manufactured imports from developing countries

	Import-penetration ratio[a]				
	1973	*1978*	*1983*	*1985*	*1987*
United States	1.1	1.8	3.0	3.4	4.6
European Economic Community	0.9	1.6	2.1	2.6	2.7
Japan	0.7	0.8	1.0	1.2	1.3

[a] Figures calculated using current prices, and given as percentages of all manufactured goods consumed domestically.

Sources: GATT, *International Trade* 1973, 1978, 1983; United Nations, *Yearbook of Industrial Statistics*; OECD, *Indicators of Industrial Activity*, various years; GATT and OECD data tapes, 1985, 1987.

It appears, then, that although Japan is not party to the MFA and has few formal barriers to imports from the developing countries (the major exception being footwear), it has increasingly lagged behind the other major industrial countries in importing manufactured goods from the developing countries. Yet, with its rapid economic growth and the accumulation of physical and human capital, Japan has approached the other industrial countries in terms of factor endowments, and one would thus have expected it to resemble them in terms of import patterns as well. The fact that the opposite has happened may be taken as an indication of the use of informal measures of protection against developing country exports in Japan.

Nor can one explain the results by the overvaluation of the US dollar relative to the European and Japanese currencies.[10] In fact, the rise of import penetration ratios decelerated in the United States during the 1983–5 period when the bulk of the dollar's appreciation occurred, and it accelerated between 1985 and 1987 when the dollar depreciated. Also, similar changes in real effective exchange rates in the European Community and Japan were accompanied by differential changes in import penetration ratios, and the appreciation of their currencies between 1985 and 1987 was accompanied by a slowdown in the rise of import penetration ratios.[11]

The observed differences in import penetration cannot be explained by the availability of natural resources or other objective factors either. This is apparent from comparisons of actual and hypothetical imports of manufactured goods from the developing countries, the latter being determined by per capita income, population, transportation costs, and the availability of natural resources. The results show Japan to be an "outlier," with actual imports falling short of hypothetical imports by a substantial margin (Balassa and Noland, 1988).[12]

4 Conclusions

We have seen that average agricultural protection has remained practically nil in the United States while rising over time in the European Community and, even more, in Japan. It further appears that manufactured imports from developing countries have increased much more rapidly, and have reached higher levels, in the United States than in the European Community and, in particular, Japan.

The US–Japan comparisons for manufactured goods do not conform to the data on the extent of nontariff barriers, as measured by the share of imports from the developing countries that are subject to such barriers. The solution to the puzzle lies in part in the fact that the data on the share of imports subject to nontariff measures are inadequate for gauging the protective effects of these measures, and in part in the fact that formal protection measures are used in the United States whereas informal measures are used in Japan.

The data of table 3.1, on the share of imports subject to nontariff measures, indicate the scope of the application of these measures but not their protective effect. Thus the fact that a particular commodity category is subject to nontariff measures is compatible with widely different levels of imports. Also, the United States has traditionally used formal measures of protection while Japan and, to a lesser extent, European countries have relied on informal measures that are difficult to evaluate.

More generally, one may explain the results obtained by reference to the openness of the US market which has generally been more hospitable to imports from developing countries than have the markets of other industrial countries, in particular Japan. Despite attempts to increase restrictions in recent years, this has continued to be the case for textiles and clothing, where developing countries have in large part gotten around the regulations by introducing new fibers, such as ramie, as well as upgrading products.

This is not to say that one should underestimate the danger of protectionist pressures in the United States. While President Reagan vetoed the highly protectionist textile bills prepared in a two-year period, protectionist pressures remain strong in Congress. It is necessary, therefore, to combat these pressures by emphasizing the economic as well as the political advantages of an open trade system for the United States. It should further be noted that the highly-indebted developing countries need markets so that they can continue servicing their loans.

Notes

* The author is indebted to Michael Finger and to Paul Meo for helpful comments on an earlier draft. However, the author alone is responsible for the contents of the chapter which should not be taken to reflect the views of the World Bank.

1 The corresponding figures for total imports are 4.9, 6.7 and 6.8 percent (GATT, 1980, pp. 33–7).
2 Nevertheless, to the extent that all, or most, developed countries apply quantitative import restrictions to the same commodities, for example textiles, their share in world trade will be lowered, thereby affecting the world trade-weighted average of nontariff measures (Balassa and Michalopoulos, 1987).
3 A case in point is the restrictions imposed on automobile imports from Japan. While US imports were set at over 20 percent of domestic sales, the French quota equals 3 percent of sales and Italy admits 11,000 automobiles from Japan.
4 Health and safety measures and technical standards may also be used with a

protective intent, but the relevant data are difficult to obtain. Furthermore, in concentrating on border measures, the discussion excludes domestic measures such as production subsidies which also bear on imports.

5 The initiation of actions against such unfair trading practices and the monitoring of imports have also been included in the calculations.

6 In the 1980–5 period, there were 26 such actions against Mexico, 16 against Brazil, six against Peru, and five each against Argentina and Venezuela. This compares with eight actions against Korea, three against Singapore and Taiwan each, and none against Hong Kong although the latter has larger exports to the United States than any Latin American country.

7 In 1980–5, the share of affirmative decisions in the total was 80 percent in Argentina, 31 percent in Brazil, 38 percent in Korea, 54 percent in Mexico, 67 percent in Peru, and nil in Singapore, Taiwan, and Venezuela; average countervailing duty rates were 15.8 percent for Argentina, 14.1 percent for Brazil, 2.4 percent for Korea, 10.8 percent for Mexico, and 22.7 percent for Peru (Nam, 1986, Table 4).

8 It should be added that the long delays of the US Administration in dealing with petitions for countervailing and dumping actions create uncertainty for US business. For example, the US Department of Commerce has still not determined 1980 Japanese dumping margins for television sets (New York Times, 14 December, 1986).

9 On the unreliability of existing estimates, see Balassa and Balassa, 1984.

10 This conclusion is supported by statistical evidence for the industrial countries, which does not show the existence of a correlation between changes in import penetration ratios and in real effective exchange rates (Balassa, 1986b).

11 With respect to Japan, this result may appear surprising in view of the oft-cited rise in Japanese imports of manufactured goods from the developing countries. But the trade data are measured in terms of US dollars, so the increase in terms of yen, relevant for making comparisons with the domestic consumption of manufactured goods, was attenuated by the appreciation of the yen *vis-à-vis* the dollar.

12 The same results have been obtained in regard to total imports as well as for primary imports.

References

Balassa, B., 1986a. Japan's trade policies toward developing countries, *Journal of International Trade and Economic Integration*, Spring, 1–19.

Balassa, B., 1986b. Japan's trade policies, *Weltwirtschaftliches Archiv*, 4, 745–90.

Balassa, B. and C. Balassa, 1984. Industrial protection in the developed countries, *World Economy*, June, 7, 179–96. (Republished as Essay 19 in Bela Balassa, *Change and Challenge in the World Economy*, London: Macmillan, 1985.)

Balassa, B. and C. Michalopoulos, 1987. The extent and the cost of protection in developed–developing country trade. In *The New Protectionist Threat to World*

Welfare, Dominick Salvatore, ed. Amsterdam: North Holland, 482–504.

Balassa, B. and M. Noland, *Japan in the World Economy*, 1988. Washington, DC: Institute for International Economics, chapter 3.

Finger, J. M., H. K. Hall, and D. R. Nelson, 1982. The Political Economy of Administered Protection, *American Economic Review*, June, 452–66.

General Agreement on Tariffs and Trade, 1973, 1978, 1983. *International Trade*, Geneva.

General Agreement on Tariffs and Trade, 1980, *The Tokyo Round of Multilateral Trade Negotiations II*, Supplementary Report, January, Geneva.

Honma, M. and Y. Hayami, 1986. Structure of agricultural protection in industrial countries, *Journal of International Economics*, February, 115–30.

Nam, C., 1986. Export-promoting policies under countervailing threats: GATT rules and practice, *Development Policy Issues Series*, Discussion Paper VPERS9, December, Washington, DC: World Bank.

New York Times, 14 December 1986.

Nogues, J. J., A. Olechowski, and L. A. Winters, 1986. The Extent of nontariff barriers to industrial countries' imports, *World Bank Economic Review*, September, 181–98.

Organization for Economic Cooperation and Development (various years), *Indicators of Industrial Activity*, Paris.

Tyers, R. and K. Anderson, 1986. Distortions in world food markets: a quantitative assessment. A background paper prepared for the 1986 World Development Report, January (mimeo). Washington, DC: World Bank.

United Nations (various years). *Yearbook of Industrial Statistics*, New York.

United Nations Conference for Trade and Development, 1985. Problems of protectionism and structural adjustment, *Report by the Secretariat*, Part I. Restrictions to Trade and Structural Adjustment, TD/B/1039, Geneva.

4

Trade Policy and the Current Account

W. Max Corden

1 Introduction

This chapter explores the relationship between trade policy and the current account. It uses the "savings-and-investment approach". In section 2, it asks whether protection can be presumed to improve a country's current account given a floating exchange rate regime. Increased protection will normally lead to appreciation and can affect savings and investment in various ways. Notably, a tariff brings in revenue, which, if not spent, can reduce the budget deficit. Because of other possible effects (e.g., higher investment in protected industries), however, the presumption that the current account will improve is not necessarily valid. In section 3 it is concluded that even if lowering protection abroad (say, in Japan) did reduce the surplus there – and there is no presumption that it would – this reduction would be likely to diminish the US current account deficit only by shrinking US investment.

In section 4, the case of a fixed exchange rate is considered. It is shown that if the country is initially in "internal balance," protection can improve the current account only because of the effects on savings and investment of the reduction in expenditure that is required to maintain internal balance when import restrictions are imposed.

Section 5 discusses one way in which the current account situation will affect protection when the exchange rate floats. A current account deficit may increase pressures for protectionism because of "conservative resistance," – that is, pressure groups in the tradable-producing sectors will resist losses in real incomes. Through the real appreciation that results, protection then tends to put at a disadvantage producers of tradables who are unable to obtain adequate protection. But it is possible that conservative resistance is stimulated not so much by a current account deficit as by real appreciation – and these may not go together – or by a boom in exports from particular countries especially if these exports are concentrated in particular products not associated with current imbalance at all.

2 Would US protection improve the US current account?

Is there any presumption that increased protection will improve a country's current account? Partial equilibrium thinking suggests that the answer is obvious: how can a reduction in particular imports not improve the current account?

Much of the thinking on this subject is still governed by the assumption of fixed exchange rates. Conceivably – just conceivably – one might regard this as relevant to the current US situation if one supposed that the US authorities wanted to avoid both further dollar depreciation and appreciation by using either direct exchange market intervention or monetary (interest rate) policy. So this fixed exchange rate case will be considered below. It is, of course, relevant for some other countries, and was the appropriate approach for the 1950s and possibly the 1960s. But the greater part of this chapter will deal with the case of an exchange rate that is flexible or that actually floats.

In analyzing this issue the guiding principle is the "savings-and-investment approach": a current account improvement requires a reduction in the budget deficit (i.e. in net public dissavings) a rise in private savings or a fall in private investment. If one wants to argue that protection must improve the current account, one must show that it must reduce the budget deficit, increase private savings or reduce private investment.[1]

Many special models could be produced where quotas or tariffs have particular impacts on the budget and on private savings and investment. The implicit assumption of the partial equilibrium approach is that the whole of an initial reduction of imports resulting from protection would be saved, so that there would be no indirect effects on purchases of other imports or on exporting to take into account. But this is just an extreme case. One possibility is that the government would not spend extra tariff revenue, so that a by-product of protection brought about by higher tariffs would be a fiscal improvement. But the most casual thought suggests that there is no general presumption that, taking various possible effects into account, the net effect on the savings–investment balance would go one way or another.[2]

Nevertheless, the consequences for the current account of the imposition of import quotas when the exchange rate floats will now be traced in some detail (though still in a highly simplified way). In this case there is no tariff revenue effect. There may be some value in showing the process by which the savings-and-investment story works, and especially the role of the exchange rate movement in that process.

In the first instance, the quantitative import restrictions might lead to higher savings. It has to be emphasized that this is not an empirical generalization but just a possibility. Restrictions are likely to lead to quota profits and some part of these might be saved. Alternatively, if domestic prices are not fully adjusted upwards or if users of imports are direct importers, excess demand for imported goods might result and, if the restrictions are expected to be temporary, some of the excess demand for the restricted products might be saved. The extra savings, and the improvement in the current account that can be shown to result, would thus be temporary. Let us suppose that the value of imports is initially reduced by $100 million and that national savings at this stage rise by $30 million, so that $70 million is available to be spent on domestic goods.

The extra savings go on the capital market and domestic interest rates decline somewhat, so that investment rises by $10 million. The rest of the extra savings replace foreign savings, so that capital inflow declines by $20 million. With imports having fallen by $100 million, if the exchange rate did not change, the overall balance of payments (current and capital account combined) would now be $80 million in surplus, assuming it was zero to start with. Reserves must thus accumulate. But in the absence of intervention the dollar must appreciate and (assuming as a first approximation that this appreciation does not itself affect savings and investment) it must appreciate sufficiently for $80 million of demand to be switched from domestic goods to imports or to exportables. Hence, finally, the current account improves to the extent of the higher savings ($30 million) less the extra investment ($10 million). It must be stressed that if there had not been any increase in saving initially, there would have been no effect on the current account at all.

The level of demand for domestic goods will stay constant: at first the increased demand was $70 million, and this was supplemented by higher investment of $10 million (assumed to have gone wholly on domestic goods), and then, as a result of the appreciation, expenditure was switched away from domestic goods to the extent of $80 million.

Various additional effects on savings and investment are possible. Essentially, these result from the redistributive effects of the combination of protection and exchange rate appreciation. Profits of newly protected industries will rise and those of other tradable producers will fall, and the savings-and-investment propensities of these two categories may differ: on balance national savings and investment could rise or fall. For example, extra investment in protected industries might be stimulated by better profit prospects if the increase in protection is expected to last for a reasonable time. This effect could well outweigh both lower investment elsewhere and changes in savings, so that the current account would worsen. The same applies to effects on tax revenue. Industries and workers that have gained from higher protection will pay more taxes, and losers will pay less. Tax revenue could thus rise or fall, and if government expenditure were held constant, the budget deficit and hence net national savings could be affected through this route. If the restrictions took the form of voluntary export restraints (which allow foreign suppliers to charge higher prices), the terms of trade would worsen and, with gains from trade being lost as well, total savings and tax revenue would be more likely to fall and the current account would be more likely to deteriorate.

All these examples indicate that there can be no general presumption about which way the overall effect of import restrictions on the current account will come out when the exchange rate floats.

3 How would reduced protection abroad affect the US current account?

It is a feature of the US Trade Act of 1988, and, in general, of popular current US approaches, that threats of protection by the United States are used to induce trading partners to open up their markets more. This then raises the interesting question of how such opening might actually affect the US current account. For example, if Japan reduced protection (explicit or implicit), how would this affect its savings–investment balance and then, through an international general equilibrium process, the US current account and thus the US savings–investment balance?

The issue can be analyzed in a two-stage process. In the first stage it can be assumed that the world interest rate is given to Japan and that the world outside Japan is willing to absorb any current account balance that emerges from Japanese savings-and-investment decisions. In other words, in the first stage Japan is assumed to be a small country on the world capital market. The second stage takes into account international general equilibrium aspects. The question in the first stage is then, what would happen to Japanese savings and investment, public and private, as a result of further market opening by Japan?

It is obvious that the analysis will be the obverse of the one just presented for the United States. Reducing Japanese import restrictions will lead to depreciation of the yen and there need be no net change in the Japanese current account at all, or it could go either way. The Japanese current account surplus could well increase because of a reduction of investment in the industries that lose some of the protection provided by formal or informal import restrictions. But let us now assume that opening up the Japanese market will indeed lead to lower private savings in Japan and thus to some reduction in the surplus. This might have resulted from the decline in the profits of the industries where protection has been reduced, not offset by higher savings in other – notably export – industries which have benefited from depreciation, and also not offset by reduced investment in the previously protected industries. The same current account result would, of course, be produced by a Japanese fiscal expansion, involving reduced net public dissavings.

The next step is to reconcile the reduced *ex-ante* Japanese current account surplus, if there is one, with a change in the current account balance of other countries, including the United States. Here the story will be told in terms of a two-country world. It will be assumed that there is no change in fiscal policy in the United States since we are interested in seeing what the effect of a Japanese market opening (or a fiscal expansion) would be by itself.

The most plausible scenario for current conditions assumes that there is little or no scope for aggregate output expansion in the United States, although the pattern of output can change. In other words, the United States is in a full capacity or "natural rate of unemployment" situation. The "Keynesian" case – where demand expansion would increase aggregate output – yields an alternative story, outlined below. With this scenario there is no particular reason to expect US savings to increase just because Japanese demand for US goods increases, because there will be no change in aggregate US output and hence incomes. Any impact on the US current account has to come through effects on investment.

Reduced Japanese savings, whether public or private, will raise world interest rates, and hence also US interest rates, and this would lead to a crowding-out of investment around the world, including investment in the United States and Japan. The key point here is that US investment is reduced, and it is through this mechanism that the US current account would improve. The higher interest rates would also reduce Japanese investment, and to that extent the eventual reduction in the Japanese current account surplus would be less than the reduction in Japanese savings. It is worth stressing that US advocates of Japanese or German fiscal expansion or of Japanese market-opening who believe that this is a way of getting a US current account improvement – one way, if not the only one – are actually proposing a process that would bring about a reduction of investment in the United States. It is hard to believe that this is what they really want.

The alternative mechanism which is often in mind – and which is probably not relevant at present, other than in the very short run – is essentially Keynesian: it is based on the assumption that output and employment in the United States can be increased as a result of extra demand. The extra Japanese net imports resulting from reduced Japanese savings, private or public, would raise demand for US goods, and hence increase output and incomes, and so generate a familiar multiplier process. This process would increase US imports – but also (if the US marginal propensity to save is positive) would produce the extra US savings that would finally yield an improvement in the US current account position.

4 How current accounts affect protection: two exchange rate regimes

So far, this chapter has dealt with the possible effects of protection on the current account. Now the obverse will be considered: the effects of a current account imbalance on protection. This is essentially a political economy issue since it is a matter of explaining why a particular policy instrument is used. Are there reasons why the existence of current account deficits might lead to more protection? Three different exchange rate regimes have to be distinguished here if the analysis is to be complete and apply not just to the United States and the major countries with floating or highly flexible exchange rates. Only the third case – the floating rate case – is relevant to the current US situation.

4.1 Fixed exchange rate

In the first case the country has a firmly fixed exchange rate in terms of some major currency or a basket. Let us assume that a current account deficit has to be reduced, for whatever reason, and that the country is initially in "internal balance." Suppose that import restrictions on their own will not generate any extra savings, nor affect investment, given that the initial situation is one of internal balance. If restrictions – which switch the expenditure pattern toward home-produced products – were imposed it would be necessary to bring about a simultaneous reduction of aggregate demand (i.e. "disabsorption") through fiscal or monetary policies to maintain "internal balance." This is standard "internal–external balance" analysis.

The way this policy prescription is usually put is that the import restrictions are targeted on external balance and the "absorption policy" on internal balance, bearing in mind that reducing absorption also reduces demand for imports and exportables and thus improves the current account. The use of import restrictions is often justified in purely partial-equilibrium terms, but this standard two-instrument two-target approach also appears to justify them, given that for historical or other reasons the market device of exchange rate adjustment has been ruled out.

But what about the savings-and-investment approach in this case? If import restrictions do not increase savings or reduce investment they cannot improve the current account. How can import restrictions then be targeted on the "external balance" objective? The answer has to be that the increase in national savings (and decrease in investment) required for the current account improvement is brought about by the associated disabsorption policies, i.e. by fiscal and monetary contraction, which are designed apparently to maintain internal balance. But then, one might ask, what is the need for import restrictions?

The answer is that the assignment of instrument to target should really be reversed. Reduction of aggregate expenditure (disabsorption) brings about the required improvement in the current account by generating the necessary increases in savings and declines in investment, but in the absence of downward flexibility of domestic prices and wages, disabsorption on its own would reduce employment and capacity utilization. It would lead to departure from internal balance. Import restrictions or similar "switching policies," notably devaluation, are needed to divert the expenditure reduction toward imports (or, more generally, toward tradeables) so as to maintain internal balance at the same time. Hence policies that reduce absorption through raising savings, public or private, or reducing investment, should be assigned to the current account target while import restrictions are assigned to the target of internal balance.[3] Of course, if the exchange rate were available as an instrument of policy, devaluation could be used to maintain internal balance.

4.2 Import restrictions versus devaluation

In the second case to be considered, the exchange rate is pegged but is available to be changed. At the present time this case covers many more countries than the previous case. The exchange rate is available as a policy instrument and governments can at various times make a choice between using import restrictions and using devaluation as "switching" devices to be associated with the disabsorption policy that is required to improve the current account. The question then is why governments prefer to use import restrictions.

Governments have a number of reasons, often implicit, for choosing import restrictions. These reasons have been much discussed in the trade theory literature. Essentially they all represent second-best, third-best or worse arguments for protection. I will just mention two examples.

Firstly, devaluation may be expected to stimulate extra exports, which are expected to be saleable abroad only at substantially lower prices. The aim of choosing import restrictions in preference to devaluation is to avoid this decline in the terms of trade. This is a version of the terms of trade argument for protection (see Corden, 1937, chapter 7, especially pp. 179–81). The best policy from the national point of view would be to tax or otherwise restrict those particular exports where terms of trade effects are expected to be significant, bearing in mind that longer-run effects of restrictions may be adverse as substitution elasticities rise over time and terms of trade effects wear off.

Secondly, nominal devaluation may be expected to lead to higher nominal wages to compensate for higher domestic prices in an environment of implicit or explicit wage indexation, and this might then negate the effects of devaluation. Of course it has to be remembered that import restrictions would also raise domestic prices; the assumption implicit in this view is that the effect of devaluation on prices and hence wages would be greater, so that import restrictions are preferred. This is the real wage rigidity (Cambridge) argument for protection, which can also be shown to be second-best or worse, and which, in any case, depends on an assumption that is not necessarily justified.[4]

It is interesting to note that the appropriate analysis of the use of import restrictions for apparently macroeconomic purposes still requires the standard trade-theory approach. The detailed analysis by trade theorists of various arguments for protection is completely relevant. Trade theory asks: what are the gains or losses from protection compared with free trade, or compared with lower protection? Here one asks: what are the gains or losses from the use of trade restrictions relative to sufficient devaluation?

5 How current accounts affect protection: conservative resistance

The third case is the one that currently applies to the United States. This time the country is assumed to have a floating exchange rate system. While there may be some exchange market intervention, it is not designed to prevent exchange rate adjustment in response to fundamental macroeconomic conditions (including fiscal policy). It was shown in section 2 that import restrictions may or may not improve the current account in such a case, depending on what happens to savings and investment, and that there is certainly no general presumption that the effect would be one way rather than another.

I shall introduce here the term "conservative resistance," rather similar to John Hicks' term "real wage resistance" introduced many years ago. I do not use the term "conservative" in the curious American sense of representing a particular ideological mixture which leads to recommendations that are often quite radical, especially in the economic sphere. I refer to the widely observed tendency for public policy measures to be used – often in response to pressures from interest groups – to moderate, if not prevent, adverse sectoral income effects of various exogenous changes, notably those originating from abroad. This can be explained in two ways.

Firstly it could be explained as a manifestation of a kind of social welfare function – the "conservative social welfare function" – which expresses the idea of protection as a form of social insurance designed to prevent severe income losses to losers, while other members of society who willingly pay the cost of protection presume that they also might need such help one day, i.e. that they also are insured (see Corden, 1987; Eaton and Grossman, 1985; and Deardorff, 1987).

Secondly, and more relevantly for the United States, pressure groups may apply more effort or resources to obtain protection when the aim is to prevent existing real incomes from declining, i.e. to conserve what exists, than when the aim is actually to obtain increases. The point is simply that the marginal utility of a dollar of income lost is, on average, greater to them than that of a dollar of income gained, so more resources will go into pressure group activities designed to maintain one dollar of income that might otherwise be lost than would go into activities designed to attain an increase of one dollar of income. It is this process – motivated by pressure groups rather than by a "conservative social welfare function" with an insurance motivation – that is best described by the term "conservative resistance."[5]

The question then is whether a shift to a large and prolonged current account deficit resulting from macroeconomic policies gives support to conservative resistance and leads to more protection even when the exchange rate floats or is clearly available as an instrument of policy. It is certainly a common view that the recent increase in protectionist pressures in the United States can be explained in these terms. A current account deficit is normally associated with an absolute or relative decline of some import-competing and export industries. It is argued that, if only the current account imbalances could be reduced, protectionist pressures would ease.[6] Apart from the influence of pressure groups, there are, of course, those who consider the current account deficit to be undesirable in its own right, i.e., to represent excessive borrowing by the United States, and who believe on the basis of fallacious partial equilibrium thinking that protection must reduce it.

Coming back to the conservative resistance motivation, one weakness of this approach should be spelled out. When a country goes into current account deficit, or when the deficit increases, other things being equal, incomes of tradable producers, whether of exportables or of import-competing products, tend to decline while those of nontradable producers tend to rise. Conservative resistance from tradable producers is then not surprising. But if protection does not improve the current account it will simply reshuffle the losses among tradable producers, essentially through the real appreciation to which it will give rise. This will be true even when the current account does improve to some extent, i.e. when import restrictions generate some extra savings, as long as there is still some real appreciation.

In practical terms, protection tends to intensify the adverse effects on those producers, mostly exporters, who are not able to obtain quotas, subsidies, and so on, or who obtain increases in protection that are, in some sense, below the average. First they lose through the current account deficit or other factors that gave rise to it, and then they lose more through the indirect effects of protection obtained by other industries. The losses will thus tend to be concentrated on exporters and on those sectors where lobbying has been less effective.

One might argue that it is not a current account deficit but rather a real appreciation that gives rise to conservative resistance initially. There is certainly some evidence that on various occasions when the dollar has appreciated significantly in real terms – i.e. when there has been a decline in competitiveness – protectionist pressures have increased (see Bergsten and Williamson, 1983; Cline, 1984; and Clifton, 1985). Recent experience shows that the exchange rate can be depreciating while the current account still worsens. Hence, when one is interested in what stimulates protectionism, the focus should possibly be not on the current account position itself but on the movement in the real exchange rate. This presumed relationship between the real exchange rate and protectionist pressures in the United States was clearly a major factor in influencing the finance ministers of the Group of Seven when they reached the Plaza Agreement of September 1985 that was designed to bring down the dollar. The question is whether the dollar depreciation that followed did moderate protectionist pressures in the United States: it is the impression of this writer that it did.

Another explanation for protectionist pressures in terms of conservative resistance may actually be more important. Any boom in exports from particular countries, especially if concentrated in particular products, is likely to give rise to such resistance. This need not be associated with current account imbalances at all since the same countries could be increasing their imports at the same time.

The boom in labor-intensive clothing and textile exports, mainly from the four Asian newly industrializing economies (NIEs), generated widespread conservative resistance from the clothing and textile industries of the "old" industrialized countries and led to the increase in protection of these industries in all developed countries. Yet the exporting countries generally did not run current account surpluses. Korea consistently ran current account deficits until 1985. Germany practiced this form of protection, not only of clothing and textiles but also of agriculture, while consistently having current account surpluses. Nor could arguments about level playing fields and retaliatory protection hold much water, bearing in mind that Hong Kong has been a uniquely free trade territory, Singapore has also been one of the world's most open economies, and Korea, while by no means a free trade country, has been no more protectionist than many other developing and possibly some developed countries.

Another example can be seen in Japan's response to the first oil shock and the reaction in other countries to the resultant Japanese export boom. The rise in oil prices put Japan into a big current account deficit in 1974, but by means of massive export expansion she was able to convert this into fairly modest surpluses of 1.6 percent of GNP by 1977 and 1.7 percent in 1978. From 1975 to 1981 the volume of Japanese exports increased by 71.5 percent, most of the increase compensating for the deterioration of her terms of trade. This generated strong conservative resistance in other countries, a resistance that was not applied to exports by the OPEC countries which were actually generating the large current account surpluses.

Here one should return to the earlier analysis of the effects of a reduction of protection by Japan. It was noted that "opening up" would not necessarily reduce Japan's savings-investment balance but would lead to more yen depreciation, or less appreciation than otherwise. In fact Japan's imports would indeed increase if protective barriers were reduced, but her exports would also increase, an inevitable consequence of the current account remaining unchanged. Hence, while the playing field might become more level, and while there would be the familiar and important gains from trade accruing both to Japan and to her trading partners, increased conservative resistance against Japanese export expansion might well result.

Notes

1 With regard to devaluation, this approach was first put clearly in Black (1959) but the basic idea originated in Alexander (1952) where the key point was made that a devaluation can only improve the trade balance if it increases "real hoarding" (i.e. savings minus investment). The extension to import restrictions was first made in Nurkse (1956). Most recently, Lawrence and Litan (1987, pp. 296–8) have explicitly put the central point here with regard to the US current account. See also Kaempfer and Willett (1987).

2 The effects of a uniform import surcharge (uniform tariff) imposed in the United States, with revenue not spent by the government, are analyzed in Klein, Pauly and Peterson (1987) using Project LINK, and in Dornbusch (1987) using the Data Resources, Inc. model. Naturally, the current account is shown to improve in these cases.

3 This was the central theme of Hemming and Corden (1958): given initial "internal balance," import restrictions cannot improve the trade balance on their own, but they are required to accompany policies that reduce absorption in order to avoid a decline in real income. This was called the "real income" approach to the use of import restrictions. See also Nurkse (1956).

4 The argument is analyzed in detail in Corden (1985, chapter 20).

5 This is, of course, only one possible explanation of relative protectionist pressures and, more generally, of the "political economy of protection." See Baldwin (1984) for a review, and also Bhagwati (1988). Takacs (1981) contains an empirical analysis of pressures for protection and of actual changes in protection in the United States as measured by escape clause actions, and this is further discussed in Feigenbaum, Ortiz, and Willett (1985).

6 It should not be assumed that the increase in "protectionist pressures" as evidenced by the 1988 trade act and the "pressures" that preceded it, has brought about an equivalent actual increase in US protectionism. In particular, the chapter by Bela Balassa in this book ("US Trade Policy Toward Developing Countries") suggests that the US market is still very open to products from developing countries, more so than the markets of Japan and the European Community.

References

Alexander, Sidney S., 1952. Effects of a devaluation on a trade balance, *IMF Staff Papers*, 2(2), 263–78.

Baldwin, Robert E., 1984. Trade policies in developed countries, in Ronald W. Jones and Peter P. Kenen (eds), *Handbook of International Economics*, vol. 1 (Amsterdam: North Holland).

Bergsten, C. Fred and John Williamson, 1983. Exchange rates and trade policy, in William R. Cline (ed.), *Trade Policy in the 1980s* (Washington, DC: International Economics).

Bhagwati, Jagdish, 1988. *Protectionism* (Cambridge, MA: MIT Press).

Black, John, 1959. A savings and investment approach to devaluation, *Economic Journal*, 69(274), 267–74.

Clifton, Eric V., 1985. Real exchange rates, import penetration and protectionism in industrial countries, *IMF Staff Papers*, 32(3), 513–36.

Cline, William R., 1984. *Exports of Manufactures from Developing Countries: Performance and Prospects for Market Access* (Washington, DC: The Brookings Institution).

Corden, W. Max, 1987. *Trade Policy and Economic Welfare* (Oxford: Oxford University Press).

Corden, W. Max, 1985. *Protection, Growth and Trade* (Oxford: Basil Blackwell).

Deardorff, Alan V., 1987. Safeguards policy and the conservative social welfare function, in Henryk Kierzkowski (ed.), *Protectionism and Competition in International Trade* (Oxford: Basil Blackwell).

Dornbusch, Rudiger, 1987. External balance correction: depreciation or protection? *Brookings Papers on Economic Activity*, 1, 249–69.

Eaton, Jonathan and Gene M. Grossman, 1985. Tariffs as insurance: optimal commercial policy when domestic markets are incomplete, *Canadian Journal of Economics*, 18, 258–72.

Feigenbaum, Susan, Henry Ortiz, and Thomas D. Willett, 1985. Protectionist pressures and aggregate economic conditions: comment on takacs, *Economic Inquiry*, 23(1), 175–182.

Hemming, M. F. W. and W. M. Corden, 1958. Import restrictions as an instrument of balance of payments policy, *Economic Journal*, 68(271), 483–510.

Hicks, John R., 1974. *The Crisis in Keynesian Economics* (Oxford: Basil Blackwell).

International Monetary Fund, 1988. *World Economic Outlook*, April (Washington, DC: IMF).

Kaempfer, William H. and Thomas D. Willett, 1987. Why an import surcharge wouldn't help America's trade deficit, *World Economy*, 10(1), 27–38.

Klein, Lawrence R., Peter H. Pauly, and Christiane Peterson, 1987. Empirical aspects of protectionism: results from project LINK, in Dominick Salvatore (ed.), *The New Protectionist Threat to World Welfare* (Amsterdam: North Holland).

Lawrence, Robert Z. and Robert E. Litan, 1987. The protectionist prescription: errors in diagnosis, *Brookings Papers on Economic Activity*, 1, 289–310.

Nurkse, R., 1956. The relation between home investment and external balance in the light of British experience, 1945–55, *Review of Economics and Statistics* (May).

Takacs, Wendy E., 1981. Pressures for Protectionism: An Empirical Analysis, *Economic Inquiry*, 19(4), 687–93.

Part II

The Developing Country Perspective

5

Trends in the Trade Policies of Developing Countries

*Anne O. Krueger**

Being asked to analyze trends in the trade policies of developing countries is not unlike being challenged to discern long-term trends in the weather. Year-to-year and decade-to-decade fluctuations in weather are large contrasted with any overall trend (and there are regional differences as well), while for developing countries, variations in policies among countries, and fluctuations in trade regimes within countries, are much greater than the variations in any long-term trend.

Nonetheless, it is worthwhile to make the effort, partly because the diversity of stances among developing countries sometimes tends to obscure common patterns, and in part because the developing countries are often perceived, and often perceive themselves, to have a common interest in the international economy. It is certainly an appropriate theme for honoring Isaiah Frank, who has done so much to increase understanding of the trade policies of developing countries and of the stake these countries have in the international economy.

Comparing the position of developing countries in the 1980s with their position in the 1950s, perhaps the sharpest change is the increasing differentiation among the developing countries. Forty years ago, it would have been a relatively simple matter to discuss a "typical" developing country with respect to structure of production, population characteristics (including life expectancy, educational attainment, and health indicators), structure of trade, and a variety of other matters. Since that time, the range of experience of developing countries has been vast: some have grown extremely rapidly, and have per capita incomes that equal or exceed the level in Italy in the mid-1950s, with the altered economy structures, population characteristics, and trade and payments regimes that go with those levels. The most prominent among these are, of course, the "newly industrializing countries" (NICs) of East Asia. Other countries have experienced rapid growth, but not to the same degree as the East Asian NICs. Another group consists of countries that have discovered large deposits of valuable natural resources, or experienced large improvements in their terms of trade (especially the oil exporters). Finally, some countries have experienced very little growth, and are little different in structure today than they were thirty or forty years ago.

While increasing diversity is perhaps the most important long-term trend among developing countries, two other phenomena are also important: there is a long-term pattern of movement toward somewhat less restrictive trade regimes among the developing countries taken as a whole; and the more successful among the developing countries have grown sufficiently, and have integrated with the world economy to such a degree, that developing countries as a whole are far more significant players in the international economy today than was the case in the 1950s.

The interplay between increased diversity, increasing liberalization, and an enhanced role in the international economy is the theme around which analysis of the changing trade policies of the developing countries can be analyzed. For the success of the East Asian NICs was associated with their decision to integrate with the international economy; that, in turn, led to efforts by many other countries to do so. Meanwhile, the increased importance of the developing countries has raised questions about their role in the international economy.

To consider these issues, this chapter is divided into three sections. The first considers the evolution of the developing countries' role in the international economy in the thirty years prior to 1980. The second section then assesses the pressures that have shaped changes in trade policies in the 1980s, and attempts an assessment of developing countries' responses to them. A third section analyzes the interests of the developing countries in the international economy in light of their current and prospective interests, and considers the concordance between those interests and the stance of the developing countries in the major international fora.

1 Evolution of the trade policies of developing countries, 1950–1980

In 1950, it would not have been much of an overgeneralization to state that developing countries were exporters of primary commodities, with most of them having exports highly concentrated in a very small number of items. Developing countries were heavily dependent on the international economy for their imports of manufactured goods other than a few artisantype items such as matches, candles, and vegetable oils. Most of them were newly independent, and nationalist leaders perceived their colonial status and concentration on a few primary commodities to have been a significant cause of their low living standards and underdevelopment.[1]

As country after country attained independence, virtually all of the independence movements had leaders who believed that colonialism had been associated with economic backwardness and that independence could be used for a rapid transformation of their economies. Thus there was a sharp political and economic imperative for economic development. But the rejection of the earlier colonial era generally implied a desire for economic development through diversification of the domestic industrial structure and reduced "dependence" on the international economy.

As is well known, most developing countries therefore adopted "import-substitution" (IS) policies, under which they used their trade regimes to protect, often by prohibiting imports, domestic production of import-competing goods. The IS policies were generally justified by appeal to the infant industry argument and/or by "export pessimism", as politicians believed that export earnings from traditional commodities could not grow rapidly enough to support desired rates of growth of real GNP.[2]

However, just as IS policies were being put in place, commodity prices fell sharply with the end of the Korean war. The consequence in many instances was a trade and payments regime much more highly restrictive than might have been put in place on infant-industry grounds alone. In part because of the suddenness with which balance of payments difficulties emerged,[3] and in part because civil servants were frequently inexperienced, the initial trade and payments restrictions were often crude, across-the-board, blunt instruments. Thus, for example, Turkey initially cut back imports in each category by an equal percentage, Chilean authorities imposed a 10,000 percent guarantee deposit charge for import licenses, and Ghanaian authorities issued import permits in the order in which applications had been received as foreign exchange became available.[4]

To make matters worse, the governments of most developing countries exhibited strong reluctance to alter their exchange rates. During the late 1950s and the 1960s, the world price level, denominated in dollars, was virtually constant. In contrast, many developing countries were experiencing inflation rates of 5–15 percent annually – moderate in contrast to many of today's rates but rapid enough to result in systematic appreciation of the real exchange rate over a period of several years. The combination of high walls of domestic protection and real appreciation naturally made exporting less attractive to domestic producers in most developing countries. The inevitable result was a decline in the share of exports of developing countries in their own real GNPs and also in world trade. For example, exports as a percentage of GNP from 1955 to 1965 fell from 7.7 to 3.9 in India, 29.7 to

Table 5.1 Total exports of developed and developing countries

Year	World	Developed countries	Developing countries: Oil importers	Developing countries: OPEC[a]
Values of exports (billions of US dollars)				
1950	60	36	19	4
1955	89	59	24	6
1960	120	84	29	7
1965	173	126	37	10
1970	291	220	52	17
1975	823	568	136	113
1980	1,892	1,240	335	297
1981	1,858	1,220	343	272
1982	1,728	1,155	329	221
1983	1,678	1,139	337	177
1984	1,778	1,215	369	164
1985	1,799	1,257	364	148
1986	1,992	1,463	371	116
1987	2,358	1,715	447	NA
Shares of world exports (%)				
1950		60.0	31.7	6.7
1955		66.3	27.0	6.7
1960		70.0	24.1	5.8
1965		72.8	21.1	5.8
1970		75.6	17.9	5.8
1975		69.0	16.5	13.7
1980		65.5	17.7	15.7
1985		69.9	20.2	8.2
1986		73.4	18.6	5.8
1987		72.7	19.0	NA

[a] OPEC members: Algeria, Ecuador, Gabon, Indonesia, Iran, Iraq, Kuwait, Libya, Nigeria, Quatar, Saudi Arabia, United Arab Emirates, and Venezuela.
Source: International Monetary Fund, 1988, pp. 122–3.

14.7 in Ghana, 20.6 to 18.5 in Peru, 16.8 to 9.8 in Mexico, and 24.1 to 18.6 in Egypt.[5]

The shares of world markets that developing countries had for their exports also fell, as can be seen from table 5.1. Developing countries' shares of total world exports declined from 34 percent in 1955 to 27 percent in 1965, while their share of world agricultural exports (table 5.3) fell from 44 to 32 percent.

However, the growth rate of the international economy was so high, with world exports more than doubling during the ten year interval, that the exports of developing countries nonetheless increased by 54 percent. Thus, the period of rapid growth for the developed countries and for the international economy was one during which the developing countries managed to grow, albeit with declining relative importance in international trade (and a declining share of world GNP).

However, in the early 1950s, Taiwan, which had had a high rate of domestic inflation and a highly restrictive trade and payments regime, undertook major policy reforms and began experiencing rapid growth of exports and of GNP. By the early 1960s, Hong Kong and Korea had embarked on similar policy reforms and growth strategies, and Singapore followed upon separating from Malaysia in 1965.

In part because of the experience of these four countries, but also because many policy makers in developing countries were observing the consequences of the excesses of their trade regimes, many countries began moderating their highly-inward-oriented trade regimes beginning in the mid-1960s. In some instances, the adoption of a crawling-peg exchange rate gave sufficient assurance to exporters that their returns would be positive to provide a reasonable stimulus to exports. Thailand abandoned multiple exchange rates in the late 1950s; Pakistan adopted a variety of export incentive schemes in the 1960s and did not thereafter return to the overall degree of restrictiveness of the trade and payments regimes of the late 1950s; and the Turkish trade and payments regime was reformed between 1958 and 1960, and it never entirely reverted to the degree of restrictiveness it previously had.

Although some countries, therefore, were already outward-oriented, and others were liberalizing significantly after the restrictiveness of the early and mid-1950s, this trend was partially offset by the increasing restrictiveness of some trade and payments regimes, especially those in Africa. Thus, by the mid-1960s, the strong trend toward increasing insulation of the developing countries from the world economy had been arrested, and there was increasing differentiation among the developing countries. However, it could not yet be said that the developing countries were increasingly integrating with the world economy.

This same mixture of trends continued into the 1970s: Indonesia had undergone significant policy reforms after 1965 and was becoming increasingly integrated with the world economy; Brazilian exports grew by an average annual rate of 40 percent (and real GNP by 10 percent) following upon policy reforms including tariff reduction and the adoption of a crawling peg in the 1967–73 period; Colombian export and GNP growth accelerated after the adoption of a crawling peg regime in 1967; and, of course, the rapid growth of the NICs accelerated. By the early 1970s, it could fairly be said that there was no longer a trend toward a diminishing share for the developing countries in world trade, although no reversal had yet started.[6]

The early 1970s, however, were a turbulent period for the world economy, with the acceleration of inflation worldwide, the commodity price boom of the 1972–4 period, and, of course, the oil price increase of 1973–4. These events in themselves further differentiated the developing countries. Even before 1973, the fortunes of oil-exporting developing countries had been somewhat brighter than others; after the oil price increase, the sharp improvement in their terms of trade resulted in their having a significantly different set of economic problems than other developing countries.[7]

This can be seen from table 5.1, where data for developing countries are split into those for oil-importing and oil-exporting countries. Oil-exporting countries doubled their share of world trade between 1970 and 1975, as the fourfold oil price increase was fully reflected in their export earnings. Interestingly, even the oil-importing developing countries were increasing their share of manufactured exports by 1975. In large part, this reflected the increasing success of the NICs, but it also reflected the move away from exceptionally restrictionist policies in a number of other countries: as already mentioned, Brazil and Colombia experienced rapid growth of export earnings in the early 1970s; Turkey once again undertook reforms of the trade regime in 1970 and began to experience more rapid growth of export earnings; exports from Thailand and Pakistan continued to grow with some rapidity; and so on.

Indeed, the governments of many developing countries reacted to the 1973–4 oil price increase by adjusting their exchange rates and increasing incentives to export; in some instances the increased export incentives were partial offsets to the incentives provided by continued protection of import-competing domestic industry, but in other instances the changes that increased export incentives were accompanied by reductions in protection to domestic import-competing industries. To be sure, other developing countries failed to respond to the deterioration in their terms of trade, either covering the increase in their current account deficits by borrowing, or else increasing the restrictionist content of the trade regime.

By the end of the 1970s, it was already questionable whether it made sense to regard developing countries as a meaningful aggregate for analysis, especially when it came to trade and exchange rate policies. Among the middle income countries, there were the successful manufacturing exporters primarily of the Far East; there were other NICs (these included Argentina, Brazil, Turkey and some Southeast Asian countries) whose manufactured exports were becoming increasingly important in world trade but whose policies were not as outward-oriented as in the Far East group and whose growth was still based largely on the protection of their internal markets; there were oil-exporting but relatively unpopulated developing countries, whose terms of trade had improved dramatically in the 1970s and who in consequence had fairly liberal trade regimes; and there were some developing countries which had experienced twenty or more years of economic growth but which were still primarily dependent on primary commodity exports (e.g. Chile, Colombia, Mexico, Thailand, Indonesia, Nigeria, Morocco). Among the low-income countries, those in South Asia continued to be heavily inward-oriented, as did many African countries which had highly restrictive trade and payments regimes, and a few others as well (Haiti, Bolivia, the Philippines, etc.).

The oil-importing developing countries had a share of world trade that remained at about 18 percent between 1970 and 1980 (table 5.1). This constancy, however, hid the fact that their share of world exports of manufactures had risen from 4 percent in 1970 to 9 percent by 1980, as can be seen in table 5.2. Reflecting the increasing diversity of the developing world, the developing countries saw their share of world exports of agricultural products continue to decline, reaching a low of 26 percent in 1980, as indicated in table 5.3. Thus the small increase in overall share was a weighted average of a declining share in agricultural exports and a growing share of manufactured exports. Given that world exports of manufactures grow more rapidly than those of agricultural commodities, this changing composition of exports by itself assured more satisfactory overall export performance, albeit with further differentiation among developing countries.

Overall, however, the period prior to 1980 can be broadly divided into two parts: the period lasting until approximately 1965, when the developing countries as a group were increasingly insulating themselves from the international economy, and the period after 1965, when they were gradually beginning to reintegrate their economies and to adopt growth strategies less dependent on import substitution. In some instances, the move toward greater integration in the late 1960s and in the 1970s was little more than a correction of some of the obvious mistakes of earlier years: exchange rates were adjusted somewhat more frequently, and there was more reliance on exchange rates and on price measures (tariffs) and less upon *ad hoc* bureaucratic decision processes including especially import licensing. Even so, by

Table 5.2 Manufactured exports of developed and developing countries[a]

			Developing countries		
Year	World	Developed countries	Oil importers	OPEC	Importers and OPEC[b]
Values of manufactured exports (billions of US dollars)					
1955	46	38			3
1960	70	58			4
1965	109	90			6
1970	202	169	7	0	
1975	518	434	38	2	
1980	1,135	937	102	8	
1981	1,125	914	114	7	
1982	1,071	864	111	7	
1983	1,085	858	125	7	
1984	1,168	916	148	7	
1985	1,221	956	160	7	
1986	1,413	1,114	184	8	
Shares of manufactured exports (%)					
1955		83			7
1960		82			6
1965		82			6
1970		84	4	0	
1975		84	7	0	
1980		83	9	1	
1983		79	12	1	
1985		78	13	1	
1986		79	13	1	

[a] Includes commodities in SITC categories 5,6,7 and 8 (rev. 2).
[b] Separate figures for oil importers and for OPEC members are not available for certain years.
Sources: UN Conference on Trade and Development (for data for 1955–65); UN Statistical Office, Department of International Economic and Social Affairs (for data for 1970–86).

Table 5.3 Agricultural exports of developed and developing countries[a]

			Developing countries		
Year	*World*	*Developed countries*	*Oil importers*	*OPEC*	*Importers and OPEC*[b]
Values of agricultural exports (billions of US dollars)					
1955	18	9			8
1960	22	12			8
1965	31	18			10
1970	41	24	12	1	
1975	104	66	28	2	
1980	200	130	52	4	
1981	200	131	52	4	
1982	188	120	52	3	
1983	184	115	52	3	
1984	186	117	54	3	
1985	177	110	52	3	
1986	224	149	57	4	
Shares of agricultural exports (%)					
1955		50			44
1960		55			36
1965		58			32
1970		59	29	2	
1975		63	27	1	
1980		65	26	2	
1982		64	28	2	
1984		63	29	2	
1986		67	25	2	

[a] Includes commodities in SITC 0 and 11 (rev. 2).
[b] Separate figures for oil importers and for OPEC members are not available for certain years.
Sources: See table 5.2.

contrast with the industrialized countries, in 1980 less developed countries (LDCs) Trade and payments regimes on average were certainly much more restrictive and there was greater variance in real exchange rates and levels of restrictiveness.

As a consequence of these trends, the developing countries as a group had lost their share of world markets, especially when those shares were calculated at constant prices so as to discount for the sharp change in oil prices. Comparing 1980 with 1955, the developing countries had a smaller share of world trade in agricultural commodities: 28 percent contrasted with 44 percent a quarter-century earlier. A partial offset was a much larger share of the world's manufactured exports than in 1950, although it was still only 10 percent and highly concentrated in origin.

Moreover, despite the reversal of earlier drifts toward increasing insulation from the world economy, developing countries continued to maintain the policy stance they had long since adopted with respect to international fora: that stance has not significantly changed during the 1980s, and will therefore be considered in section 3.

2 Evolution of trade and payments regimes in the 1980s

In light of the continuing differentiation among developing countries over the preceding decades, it is even more difficult to generalize about trends in trade and exchange rate policies during recent years than during the thirty years prior to 1980. Indeed, diversity has become so great that the only way to proceed is to identify groups of countries among which common patterns seem to emerge. These patterns, however, have been shaped in large part by the evolution of the international economy in the 1980s, as the policies of many countries have been formulated in near-crisis conditions.

The broad thrust of the international economy in the 1980s has been to render the environment much harsher and much less permissive of policy mistakes than was the case in earlier decades. As is well known, the oil price increase of 1979 was followed by deflationary policies on the part of the major industrial countries, which resulted in a prolonged and severe worldwide recession, with falling commodity prices and high nominal and real rates of interest. Although oil prices remained close to their post-1979 levels until the mid-1980s, the prices of other major primary commodities fell sharply, often in real terms, to the lowest levels experienced since the 1930s. Simultaneously, just as export earnings were falling, high nominal and real interest rates associated with the tight monetary policies of the major industrial countries increased the carrying cost of debt sharply.[8]

Although growth of the international economy resumed in 1984, the rate of worldwide inflation fell sharply and commodity prices remained at much lower levels than those associated with earlier recovery periods. Accompanying this slowdown, at least until 1987, the rate of growth of the value of world trade was significantly lower than it had been in the 1960s and 1970s. The combination of falling commodity prices, high interest rates, and domestic economic policies, which was sustainable only through large current account deficits, led to debt crises for a number of developing countries.

By late 1982, after Mexico (where there were no significant terms-of-trade problems and where fiscal excesses were so obvious as to be unarguable) announced her inability to service her debt,[9] commercial banks became extremely reluctant to continue lending to most of their other developing country borrowers. The typical consequence was the macroeconomic necessity to undertake a sharp and drastic reduction in the size of the current account deficit. Usually, the urgency of the problem resulted in quick action, with at least some new resources from the international organizations and the commercial banks accompanying changes in domestic economic policies. Entailing as they did the necessity for very sharp cutbacks in expenditures relative to income, these emergency policy packages often contained strong measures impacting on the trade and payments regimes.

2.1 Groups of countries

The evolution of the trade regimes of various developing countries during the 1980s was a function of the initial situations in those countries, the impact of the worldwide recession and associated global changes upon them, and the economic policies the authorities were in any event trying to pursue. Several broad groups of countries can be distinguished:

1 those that had experienced enough earlier growth, and were sufficiently outward-oriented, that they could adjust relatively rapidly and resume growth;
2 those countries that were in the process of policy reform at the start of the 1980s;
3 those countries that had been severely affected by the worldwide recession and the debt crisis, and then made major efforts at policy reform;
4 those countries that were severely affected by the evolution of the international economy and did not achieve appropriate reforms;
5 the oil-exporting countries; and
6 countries which, by virtue of the earlier insulation from the international economy, were not significantly affected by the turbulent international environment and could therefore simply continue on their earlier policy and growth path.

As will be seen, even this six-way characterization of countries does not do justice to the variety of experiences. Argentina, for example, started the 1980s with high levels of foreign exchange reserves, a healthy export position, and a reasonably low level of international debt. The problems that arose during the 1980s would probably have arisen in any imaginable international economic environment, although the worldwide recession no doubt intensified the problems and made resolution more difficult. Argentina is thus classed in the fourth group.

In this section, the fortunes of each group of countries are briefly described. Thereafter, some broad trends which seem to emerge are examined.

2.1.1 The outward-oriented, rapid-growth countries This group consists of the East Asian NICs (Hong Kong, Korea, Singapore, and Taiwan), several Southeast Asian countries (Malaysia and Thailand), and Colombia,[10] which have gradually liberalized their trade and payments regimes and which were able to maintain their liberalization during the 1980s. As is well known, these countries were severely affected by the worldwide recession, and most of them are oil importers and were thus adversely affected by the oil price increase. Nonetheless, they rapidly adjusted their domestic economic policies and also their trade and payments regimes, realigning their real exchange rates to offset the deterioration in their terms of trade associated with the oil price increase. By 1983, they had all been able to resume economic growth. Indeed, with the exception of Singapore, their growth rates in the mid-1980s have been similar to those of earlier decades.

The East Asian NICs all had strong incentives to export throughout the past several decades. They had also been liberalizing their import regimes, although only Hong Kong could have been described as having had a regime close to free trade. This gradual liberalization continued in the early 1980s, but at a slower pace.

By the mid-1980s, however, first Taiwan and then South Korea incurred large and growing current account surpluses. These surpluses could be attributed in part to the shift in worldwide economic conditions: lower interest rates and falling oil prices helped, as did dollar depreciation (as they were tied to a currency basket with heavy weighting for dollars). By the mid-1980s, the American authorities were pressing for exchange rate appreciation and for liberalization of the trade and payments regimes.[11] Partly because the current account balance placed unwanted inflationary pressures on their economies, and partly in response to American pressures, the NICs took significant measures to accelerate the pace of trade liberalization. In the Korean case, for example, the average tariff rate should decline to 7 percent by the end of 1988. The impact of nontariff barriers to imports has been reduced, and further reductions are anticipated.

Interestingly, the pattern of protection in Korea, and to a lesser degree in Taiwan (which does not appear to have such a significant comparative disadvantage in agriculture) now bears a closer resemblance to that of developed countries than it does to other developing countries: protection levels for domestic agriculture are very high contrasted with the protection accorded to manufacturing.[12]

While there is considerable scope for further trade liberalization in the NICs, the NICS rely on monetary, fiscal, and exchange rate policy for regulation of their international transactions. Certainly at least since the early 1980s, their policy stance has been to reduce remaining protection, although they, like other countries, encounter opposition from domestic producers.

2.1.2 Countries already in the process of policy reform in 1980–1981

Several countries had begun policy reforms in the late 1970s. These included Chile, China, Sri Lanka, and Turkey.[13] In the Sri Lankan case, a new government had come to power in 1978 with an apparent mandate to dismantle the regime of controls on both internal and external transactions that had earlier been put in place.[14] Although Sri Lanka, like all other oil-importing developing countries, suffered a sharp deterioration in her terms of trade in the early 1980s, there was little outstanding external debt, and the momentum for trade and for payments liberalization begun in 1978–9 continued into the 1980s. By the mid-1980s, the Sri Lankan trade regime was reasonably open, although some import licensing remained. The exchange rate was adjusted periodically to take into account differentials in inflation.

Turkey, likewise, had undertaken a far-reaching economic policy reform program starting in January 1980. After years of import substitution, the exchange rate was devalued sharply, and thereafter adjusted almost daily in line with inflation differentials. During the early 1980s, Turkey was able to continue the reforms, and the restrictiveness of the trade regime diminished sharply as import licensing requirements were reduced and moves toward currency convertibility were undertaken. Partly because the more realistic exchange rate provided a significant added incentive to exports, export growth was reasonably rapid during the first half of the 1980s, thus permitting liberalization to continue. By 1985, the negative list (of prohibited imports) was abolished, and the number of items subject to import licensing was reduced sharply.

In Chile, also, the authorities had moved to liberalize the trade regime in the 1970s, adjusting the exchange rate in line with changes in relative inflation rates. By the late 1970s, the Chilean authorities had reached a point where the highest tariff (except for automobiles) was 10 percent and Chile could be described as having had one of the most liberal trade regimes among developing countries. The early 1980s were a difficult period economically, with a sharp drop in copper prices and a period during which the currency appreciated 30 percent in real terms. The ensuing inability to service debt voluntarily led to a sharp devaluation and a reimposition of higher tariffs, ranging to 35 percent. However, by 1985, the momentum toward trade and payments liberalization had been restored, and now the highest tariff is once again 10 percent with the exchange rate and monetary and fiscal policy being relied upon to maintain payments balance.[15]

Finally, as is well known, Chinese reforms began in the late 1970s. To date, these reforms have centered on domestic policies, although the extreme isolation of China from the international economy has diminished. While the Chinese trade and payments regime is still highly controlled, it must be counted as one that has been significantly liberalized during the course of the 1980s as Chinese exports and imports have grown even more rapidly than GNP.

2.1.3 Heavily indebted countries with major reform efforts As already mentioned, categorization of countries is difficult, and some might argue that Chile should be placed in this category, rather than with the countries that had already begun a reform effort. Moreover, many structural adjustment programs are in progress, and the verdict is not yet in as to whether they are sufficiently far-reaching and sustainable so that they will continue, or whether, indeed, balance of payments crises or other pressures will result in a reversal of the reforms thus far instituted.

Nonetheless, there are a few countries for which reform efforts in response to the debt crisis and domestic economic difficulties appear to have been sufficiently far-reaching for there to be a reasonable basis for optimism. These include Bolivia, Mexico, Uruguay, and, with a smaller degree of confidence, a few African countries.

In all of these cases, earlier policies had been highly inward looking with large macroeconomic imbalances. High rates of inflaton had not been accompanied by commensurate exchange rate changes, and balance of payments difficulties had ensued except where exogenous shifts (such as Mexican oil) obscured the problem. All have adopted fairly far-reaching policy reform packages, with considerable emphasis on exchange rate realignment and liberalization of the import regime. For this group of countries, the trade and payments regime is considerably more liberal than it was in the early 1980s; in some instances (such as Mexico) there was an intervening period during which the restrictiveness of the import regime increased, but those moves were more than offset by later liberalization.

2.1.4 Countries making less effective structural adjustment efforts[16] Most of the heavily indebted countries initially responded to their debt-servicing difficulties by imposing or tightening quantitative restrictions over imports. In many instances, these countries were ones that had previously been liberalizing their trade regimes.

The initial response to economic difficulties was to reverse the trends of earlier years, sometimes very sharply. Almost all heavily indebted countries reinstated or intensified quantitative restrictions in response to the debt crisis, although many also adjusted the exchange rate. A large number of those countries have since undertaken some reform efforts which have liberalized their trade and payments regimes. In some instances (Jamaica,

Morocco and Costa Rica), it can be argued that the trade regime now is more liberal than it was at the outset of debt difficulties. However, in others (Ecuador and the Philippines, for example) the regimes do not yet appear to have reattained the degree of openness they had in 1980.

Most of the reform programs have included significant realignments of the exchange rate, and many have also entailed some degree of reform of the trade regime, including switching from reliance on quantitative restrictions to tariffs and often lowering the maximum heights of tariffs. To date, however, the sustainability of these programs has not been assured, and some countries have reversed the direction of policy when confronted with new economic difficulties.

2.1.5 Oil-exporting developing countries Many of the nonpopulous oil exporting countries have conducted their trade and exchange rate policies for purposes unrelated to balance of payments management since the early 1970s. For this group of countries, foreign exchange reserves and export earnings have been so large – at least until very recently – that the trade and payments regimes of these countries have been based on domestic considerations.

The populous oil exporters (e.g. Nigeria, Venezuela, Cameroon, Egypt, Indonesia) represent a more interesting group. Perhaps the most significant feature is that each of them can be placed in one of the other categories – their oil does not appear to make them different in significant ways.

Nigeria's experience, for example, is not dissimilar to that of the other countries included in the fourth group. In Nigeria, oil exports permitted the use of an unrealistic exchange rate until the early 1980s, and Nigeria's debt difficulties since that time have been similar to those of other heavily indebted countries. Venezuela, like Nigeria, has experienced debt-servicing and other difficulties similar to other heavily indebted countries.

Indonesia, by contrast, appears to resemble countries in the first group, although import restrictions (to protect domestic industry) make the Indonesian economy more closed than the economies of other Southeast Asian countries. Indonesia was, of course, among the early countries to liberalize her trade and payments regime (in the 1960s), but has become somewhat more protectionist in the 1980s. Even so, devaluation and exchange rate management has been an important component of the Indonesian policy response to the falling oil prices of the past several years.

2.1.6 Countries with relatively unchanged policies in the 1980s Finally, there are some countries which have been able to maintain the policies of earlier years into the 1980s with little change. Most notable in this group of countries are those in the South Asian subcontinent – India, Pakistan, Bangladesh, and Nepal. None of those countries was heavily indebted at the start of the 1980s. All were following relatively inward-oriented development strategies. All were adversely affected by the oil price increase of 1979 and the recession of 1980–3.

Nonetheless, by virtue of their relatively conservative monetary and fiscal policies, these countries were able to continue on paths of relatively sluggish growth. Indeed, several of them undertook limited measures to liberalize their trade regimes: India, for example, significantly reduced the applicability of import licensing restrictions, and attempted in other ways to reduce the complexity of the licensing process.

2.2 Trends in trade and exchange rate policy

Perhaps the most significant trend among developing countries in the 1980s has been their increasing reliance on exchange rate adjustment in response to balance of payments difficulties. This increased reliance has certainly permitted most developing countries to have more liberal trade and payments regimes than would have been possible without altered policies for exchange rate management.

Some indication of the extent to which reliance on exchange rates has increased can be gleaned from summary data from the International Monetary Fund. As of March 1982, Costa Rica was the only developing country to maintain an "independently floating" exchange rate arrangement; by 1985, Bolivia, the Dominican Republic, Jamaica, the Philippines, Uruguay, Zaire and Zambia had joined the list.[17] Moreover, by the mid-1980s, countries that continued to peg their exchange rates were generally more willing to alter them in response to payments pressures than they had earlier been. In 1985, the Fund estimated that real exchange rates of developing countries had depreciated by about 13 percent on a trade-weighted basis, and noted the greater willingness of developing countries to use exchange rate adjustments.[18]

Given that some part of the earlier excessive restrictiveness of trade and payments regimes was the result of extreme currency overvaluation, the increased willingness to conduct realistic exchange rate policies in itself represents an important trend with respect to the trade regimes of developing countries.

Perhaps even more interesting and remarkable, however, is that it is by no means clear that the trade policies of developing countries are any more restrictive in 1987 than they were at the end of the 1970s! As the brief sketch of these trade policies set forth above should have indicated, it is easier to point to cases where trade regimes have further liberalized than it is to point to cases where regimes have continuously become more restrictive. Certainly, at the end of 1983, one would have concluded that the earlier trend toward greater liberalization had been reversed. However, given the significant number of countries which have since restored their earlier liberalization measures, it seems reasonable to conclude, as of 1988, that the earlier trend toward liberalization was certainly stalled during the recession of 1980–3, but that it then resumed course.

This conclusion is borne out by the data in table 5.1. As can be seen, the oil-importing developing countries had shares of world exports that continued to rise in the 1980s, reaching 20.2 percent in 1985. To be sure, this partly reflected reduced shares of oil exporters, but the overall direction of change is nonetheless clear.

3 The policies of developing countries toward the world trading system

There are few who would quarrel with the proposition that more rapid growth of an open, international economy will lead to more rapid growth for the developing countries, *given* their trade and payments regimes. Moreover, for developing countries as a group, an open multilateral system is essential if those countries basing their growth strategies on an outward-oriented set of trade policies are to be able to achieve anything like the same degree of success attained by the outward-oriented countries in the 1960s and 1970s. An even stronger statement can be made: in the unlikely event that the industrial countries were to restrict the rate of growth of real exports from the developing countries to, say, the rate of growth of real GNP in the industrial countries, that would severely dampen the growth prospects of the developing countries as a group.

To be sure, developing countries with outward-oriented trade policies will in all world economic circumstances generally have better economic performance than those with highly restrictive import-substitution regimes.[19] Nonetheless, there can be little doubt that developing countries now have a strong stake in the GATT system. And, as indicated by their increasing share in world trade, they should have an increasingly strong voice and should participate more fully in GATT activities.

Historically, however, the developing countries insisted upon "special and differential" treatment (see Wolf, 1987, for an analysis) within the GATT. This insistence was based upon the ideology discussed in section 1, under which export pessimism, and the belief that the manufacturing industries of developing countries could not compete with established industries in developed countries. In the 1950s and 1960s, the stance of the developing countries was consistent with their policies toward their trade and payments regimes.

As the policies of developing countries have changed, however, their stance vis-à-vis the GATT has changed much more slowly. Whereas the reality of their policies in the 1950s was consistent with their actions in GATT (however wise or ill-advised these policies were), the insistence on special and differential treatment in the 1980s, with all that it entails, is clearly inconsistent with the increased importance of market access, and the increased ability of the developing countries to compete.

To be sure, a few of the advanced NICs have indicated a greater interest in the Uruguay Round of trade negotiations, and have recognized the importance of a successful outcome to them. However, they have by and large voiced their hopes for a successful round but have failed to offer significant reductions of their own trade barriers in return.[20]

GATT negotiations result in reciprocal reductions of trade barriers. These reciprocal reductions are then mutually "bound", to assure trading partners of the permanence of the cuts. Developing countries, by staying aloof from the major GATT negotiations and by retaining special and differential treatment and simultaneously citing the balance of payments exception to justify their continued protection, have been unable to negotiate for reciprocal benefits. Their trend toward increasing liberalization has been unilateral.[21]

Thus, despite the very significant trend toward increased liberalization of trading regimes by developing countries, little has been gained by way of negotiated liberalization on the part of the developed countries. During the 1960s and 1970s, failure to negotiate reciprocal concessions was probably not important, due both to the small amount of trade carried on by the developing countries and to the fact that the industrial countries were in any event undertaking major liberalization of their trade and payments regimes.

In the 1980s, however, the failure of developing countries actively to negotiate could be far more costly: protectionist pressures in the developed countries are probably stronger than they were in earlier decades, and the larger share of the developing countries makes them vulnerable to protectionist pressure.

Hopefully, the evolution of the Uruguay Round will entail sufficient participation by developing countries, and enough success from that participation, to demonstrate the gains to be achieved from more active participation in GATT activities in support of an open, multilateral system. Clearly, from the viewpoint of the developing countries, as well as the industrial countries, the success of the Uruguay Round is vitally important.

Notes

* I am indebted to Pablo Barahona for research assistance for this chapter.

1 Even in those countries that had been independent throughout the nineteenth and early twentieth centuries, there was a strong feeling of economic dependence on the industrial countries.
2 For a discussion of export pessimism, see Bhagwati (1988, beginning at p. 89).
3 Many developing countries had entered the postwar era with large foreign exchange reserves built up during the Second World War. In the early postwar years, reserves had been run down as unanticipated balance of payments deficits were incurred at fixed exchange rates. In many countries, the decline in commodity prices took place at about the same time that reserves were exhausted, which further accentuated the sharp increase in pressure that was felt by the authorities to restrict incipient balance of payments difficulties.
4 These and other episodes are documented in the series of studies undertaken by the National Bureau of Economic Research on Foreign Trade Regimes and Economic Development. See Bhagwati (1978) and Krueger (1978) for summaries.
5 Data are from International Monetary Fund (1988, country pages).
6 See Krueger (1978, p. 38, Figure 2–1) for visual confirmation of this trend.
7 There were, of course, at least two different groups of oil exporting countries: the relatively sparsely-populated Middle Eastern oil exporters, and the populous oil-exporting countries. This latter group included such diverse countries as Indonesia, Egypt, Nigeria, and Cameroon. For an analysis of the "Dutch Disease", associated with the problems experienced by oil exporting countries, see Corden and Neary (1982).
8 An analysis of the underlying factors leading to this constellation of circumstances would go far beyond the topic of this chapter. Suffice it to say that a combination of tight monetary and easy fiscal policy in the United States, with large accompanying fiscal and current account deficits, must certainly be assigned a large responsibility. For a discussion, see Frankel (1988).
9 See Kraft (1984) for an account of the onset of the Mexican debt crisis.
10 Colombia is difficult to characterize. The country was able to honor all her debt-servicing obligations throughout the 1980s, in part because there had been earlier liberalization and strong export growth, and in part because borrowing had been limited. By the mid-1980s, however, trade restrictions were tightened somewhat. See Laird and Nogues (1988) for an analysis, and a difference in classification.
11 See Young (1988) for an account of the Korean trade liberalization and the pressures on the Koreans.
12 See Anderson and Hayami (1986) for further analysis.
13 Brazil encountered balance of payments difficulties late in 1980 and undertook a variety of measures early in 1981 which probably would, under normal world conditions, have permitted restoration of sustainable balance of payments aggregates. In the event, the severity of the recession and Brazil's level of indebtedness led to major debt-servicing difficulties, and Brazil is therefore placed in the fourth category.
14 See Fernando (1987) for an analysis of the shift.
15 See *New York Times*, 10 October 1988, p. 4.
16 Most of the categorizations in this section are from Laird and Nogues (1988).
17 Data are from International Monetary Fund (1982, 1986).

18 International Monetary Fund (1986, p. 5) The Fund noted continuing import liberalization in 1986 and 1987. See also the classification of arrangements as of 31 March 1988 (International Monetary Fund, 1988, p. 11).

19 See Krueger (1983) for documentation.

20 See Young (1988) for a discussion of the Korean case.

21 The absence of a mechanism for obtaining "credit" for unilateral liberalization is a consequence of appeal to the balance of payments clause for invocation of tariffs.

References

Anderson, K., and Hayami, Y., 1986. *The Political Economy of Agricultural Protection*, Sydney: Allen and Unwin.

Bhagwati, Jagdish., 1978. *Foreign Trade Regimes and Economic Development: Anatomy and Consequences of Exchange Control*, Ballinger Press for the National Bureau of Economic Research.

Bhagwati, Jagdish, 1988. *Protectionism*, Cambridge, MA: MIT Press.

Corden, W. M. and Neary, J. P., 1982. Booming sector and de-industrialization in a small open economy", *Economic Journal*, 93, 825–48.

Fernando, Nimal, 1987. The Political Economy of Mahaweli (mimeo).

Frankel, Jeffrey A., 1988. International capital flows and domestic economic policies, in Martin Feldstein, ed., *The United States in the World Economy*, Chicago: University of Chicago Press.

General Agreement on Tariffs and Trade, 1987/8. *International Trade 1987/88*, Sections 1 and 2 Geneva.

International Monetary Fund, 1982, 1988. *Exchange Arrangements and Exchange Restrictions*, Washington, DC: IMF.

International Monetary Fund, 1988. *International Financial Statistics*, Washington, DC: IMF.

Kraft, Joseph, 1984. *The Mexican Rescue*, New York: Group of Thirty.

Krueger, Anne O., 1978. *Foreign Trade Regimes and Economic Development: Liberalization Attempts and Consequences*, Ballinger Press for the National Bureau of Economic Research.

Krueger, Anne O., 1983. *Trade and Employment in Developing Countries*, vol. 3. Chicago: University of Chicago Press.

Laird, Sam and Nogues, Julio, 1988. Trade policies and the debt crisis (mimeo), August, Washington, DC: World Bank.

New York Times, 10 October 1988, p. 4.

United Nations Conference on Trade and Development, *Handbook of International Trade Statistics* (various issues), New York: UN.

United Nations Statistical Office, Department of International Economic and Social Affairs, *International Trade Statistics Yearbook* (various issues), New York: UN.

Wolf, Martin, 1987. Differential and more favorable treatment of developing countries and the international trading system, *World Bank Economic Review*, September.

Young, Soo Gil, 1988. The Republic of Korea and the Uruguay Round of multilateral trade negotiations. Presented at the Rockefeller Foundation Conference on the Multilateral Trade Negotiations and the Developing Countries, 15–16 September, Washington, DC.

6

Responses of Developing Countries to Trade Protectionism in Industrial Countries

*Enzo Grilli**

Introduction

Whether as an engine or a handmaiden of growth, the benefits of trade have found recognition in development theory and practice, despite the difficulties encountered in measuring them and the uncertainty that still exists on how best to exploit the contribution that exports, particularly of manufactures, can make to industrialization in developing countries. Similarly, some disagreement still remains both at the theoretical and the policy levels on the role that domestic trade policies play in promoting exports, and on the relative importance of external economic conditions versus domestic policies (Diaz-Alejandro 1975, Lewis 1980, Streeten 1982, Helleiner 1986, Prebish 1983, Singer and Gray 1988, versus Bhagwati and Srinivasan 1978, Balassa 1971, 1978a, 1985, Krueger 1978, 1980, 1983, 1984).

Nonetheless, the turnaround in attitudes regarding trade and the changes in actual trade policy that have occurred in a large number of developing countries in the 1980s are very significant. Trade regimes have been substantially liberalized in the countries of the southern cone of Latin America, where earlier liberalization efforts met serious reversals in the late 1970s. Apart from Chile and Uruguay, far-reaching trade reforms were implemented in recent years in Bolivia, Costa Rica, Mexico, and Jamaica. Trade liberalization has also progressed significantly in several African countries, including the Ivory Coast, Senegal, Madagascar, Ghana, Nigeria, and Morocco. And progress has been made in such countries as Pakistan, Tunisia, Colombia, Mauritius, and Kenya.

As a result of the changes that occurred in the trade policy orientation of many developing countries, increasing importance is now being paid to the price incentives that appear to be necessary to ensure both the domestic supply of exportable goods and the external competitiveness of exports. Real exchange rate policies have thus become the object of close attention in most developing countries.

Apart from the increasing consensus, built upon a wide range of suggestive empirical evidence, on the positive role of trade in the growth process (Michaely 1977, Heller and Porter 1978, Balassa 1978b, 1981, 1985, Tyler 1981, Feder 1982, Nishimizu and Robinson 1984, Kavoussi 1984, 1985, Ram 1985, Jung and Marshall 1985), in the 1980s powerful realities brought home to developing country policymakers the vital importance of exports. Briefly, these included a halt in private bank lending, an increase in debt service caused by rising real interest rates, and the failure of many of the sheltered (often publicly financed) industries in developing countries to produce efficiently and compete effectively with imports in domestic markets or with competitors' goods in export markets. In a highly constrained payments situation, the contribution of exports to increased purchasing power and, more fundamentally, to greater economic efficiency at home could no longer be disregarded.

Two questions, however, have regularly surfaced in the debate over the potential benefits of the policy prescriptions aimed at increasing exports. These questions are somewhat interrelated. The first has to do with the so-called "fallacy of composition," or with the limits of the "small-country" assumption. The second concerns the constraints that trade protectionism might pose to export-oriented growth strategies followed by developing countries. The link between the two questions lies in the relationship between market penetration and protectionism.

Those who harbor reservations about the wisdom of generalized export-led growth policies in developing countries point to the special circumstances that allowed the newly industrializing countries (NICs) to succeed in generating high rates of growth in exports of manufactured products and in penetrating markets in developed countries. Their success, according to this point of view, was made possible by buoyant external demand in the 1960s and early 1970s, decreased trade protectionism during a critical phase of their industrial development, multilateralization of production, and, generally, by the very fact that these countries were the first to industrialize and export manufactured goods. This view holds that the experience was unique, and that the policy model should not thus be assumed to be automatically replicable. (Taylor 1982, Streeten 1982, Cline 1982, 1984).

Followers of the same export-based strategy would now have to contend with more limited market opportunities as well as with higher risks of protectionist actions than their predecessors. What was good for a handful of "first comers" would not necessarily and automatically be good for the "followers". As pointed out by Cline (1982, 1984), there would appear to be limits to the overall market penetration that exports of manufactures from developing countries can hope to achieve. Not all developing countries can thus expect to reach the same level of export-based industrialization as the NICs. In other words, perfect price-elastic world demands may well be faced by developing countries one by one, but not by all of them at the same time. This is the "fallacy of composition" error. The available empirical evidence on the price elasticities faced by developing country exports of manufactures in world markets tends to underline the importance of this argument. Even singly, developing countries seem to face a demand schedule for their manufactures that is much less than infinitely price-elastic (Faini, Clavijo, and Senhadji 1988).

Analysts who discount the practical relevance of these arguments often point to the success achieved by the second generation of developing countries; these so-called newly exporting countries (NECs) have developed a substantial domestic capacity to export manufactures (Havrylyshyn and Alikhani 1982, Havrylyshyn and Wolf 1983, Balassa 1984). This group bases its optimism about the room for growth that would still exist on the low share of industrial country markets that developing countries hold in most categories of manufactures (Hughes and Waelbroeck 1981, Hughes and Krueger 1984, Balassa and Balassa 1984). In addition, these observers point to the potential for export expansion held by intra-industry trade between developed and developing countries and to the relatively long time it takes for countries to industrialize. The risks of a "bunching up" of exports of manufactures from developing countries, therefore, seems low to them (Balassa 1988).

Generally speaking, these analysts are also inclined to believe that the key obstacles to successful export development are more likely to be found in domestic supply constraints and related policy failures than in external market bottlenecks. As a result, they emphasize the importance of domestic policies in creating the right conditions for the growth of export supply and ultimately for successful export expansion.

The second point concerns restrictive trade policies introduced by industrial countries to slow down imports from rapidly industrializing developing countries. The non-tariff barriers (NTBs) erected by industrial countries, moreover, seem more difficult to counter within the established legal framework governing international trade, since they purportedly lack transparency and are selectively imposed. They are also more difficult to oppose through autonomous national actions, since single developing countries have only a very limited capacity to retaliate against industrial countries that selectively use NTBs.

Since the early 1970s trade protectionism has been increasingly based on non-tariff and, at times, on non-price measures. This tendency is by now well documented (Nowzad 1978, Olechowski and Sampson 1980, Anjaria, et al. 1981, Nogues, Olechowski, and Winters 1984, Balassa and Balassa 1984, Finger and Olechowski 1987, Kostecki 1987, Grilli 1988a). Analysis of the trends in non-tariff protection by industrial countries since the early 1970s has also shown that the new protectionism, which was born as an intra-industrial-country phenomenon, has spread substantially in country and product coverage. It now affects the exports of a number of developing countries and a variety of labor- or resource-intensive products of special interest to them.

Protectionism in industrial countries

Voluntary export restraints (VERs) are the dominant instrument for regulating trade in textiles and clothing between industrial and developing countries. Under the umbrella of the multi-fiber arrangements (MFAs) and various other bilateral agreements, more than 100 VERs currently regulate developing country exports of textiles and clothing to industrial countries. In addition, by 1986 there were at least 99 additional VERs covering other types of exports, up from about a dozen in the early 1970s. Of these, 49 concerned exports from developing countries; Korea, Brazil, and Taiwan were targeted most often. Aside from agriculture, these VERs applied primarily to steel, electronics, footwear, transport equipment, and textiles and clothing that fell outside the scope of the MFAs (Boonekamp 1987, Kostecki 1987).[1]

In addition to formal and informal quotas, licenses, import prohibitions, and other measures that directly limit imports, a variety of border measures are increasingly used to restrain undesired imports – from monitoring prices and quantities to ascertaining the "fairness" of foreign trade practices. Surveillance measures, antidumping and countervailing-duty actions, and investigations of "unfair" trading practices have assumed increasing importance in industrial countries. Moreover, several countries have liberally invoked procedures such as safeguard actions and escape clauses originally designed to temporarily slow import growth to avoid undue domestic disruptions.

Although this latter group of non-tariff barriers has varying effects on trade that are not strictly comparable, the increased use of non-tariff regulations has become an important indicator of trade policy trends in the past 15 years. Not only have these measures been increasingly employed in the United States, the European Community, Australia, and Canada, but they are targeted at a growing number of developing countries, particularly the

NICs. They have been used specifically against labor- and resource-intensive products in which developing countries have greater comparative advantage (see table 6.1).

The causes of protectionism in the 1970s and 1980s have been intensively studied. The political economy of protection has proven fruitful in explaining the inter-industry structure of trade and other public assistance in most developed countries (Pincus 1975, Caves 1976, Cable and Rebelo 1980, Glismann and Weiss 1980, Tharakan 1980, Anderson and Baldwin 1981, Koekkoek, Kol, and Mennes 1981, Finger, Hall, and Nelson 1982, Grilli and LaNoce 1983, Ray and Marvel 1984, Baldwin 1985a, Anderson and Garnaut 1987). Demand for trade protection, or more generally for government assistance, has been shown to depend on such factors as the size of the industry, its labor intensity, its concentration at the firm level, its regional location, the strength of foreign competition, and the overall state of the domestic economy. The supply of trade protection, instead, depends on the conditions influencing the political costs of protection. Among them one finds education levels, the political sophistication of the electorate, the quality of information systems available to the public, the intellectual climate of the country (including its traditions of government intervention) and prevailing institutional arrangements in the field of trade policy.

The dynamics of non-tariff protection in the major industrial areas have also been analyzed (Takacs 1981, Salvatore 1987, Grilli 1988b). The results confirm the importance of both cyclical and structural factors as determinants of changes in non-tariff protection. Real exchange rate movements, among the former, and shifts in comparative advantage, among the latter, have been shown to affect the market penetration of imports. Demand for protection, in turn, is influenced by market penetration and by the cycle in economic activity in the importing country. The greater the market penetration and the more unfavorable the domestic economy, the faster the demand for non-tariff protection grows.

A more controversial point concerns the consequences of NTBs for developing countries. Among economists there are those who take a rather relaxed view of the new brand of protectionism (Gard and Riedel 1980, Hughes and Waelbroeck 1981, Balassa and Balassa 1984, Hughes and Krueger 1984, Riedel 1984, and point either to the continued growth of developing country exports of manufactures in the 1970s and 1980s or to the gap between the apparent and the actual bite of the new protectionism (Baldwin 1982, 1985b, Bhagwati 1987, 1988). In Bhagwati's words, the "(protectionist) dog barked but did not bite." The intruders were far too nimble! Developing countries, in other words, got around the barriers.

Others look at the protectionist phenomenon as much more worrisome and highlight the risks incurred by developing countries in relying on export-

Table 6.1 Geographical and sector distribution of monitoring actions initiated in the EC and USA which ended with the adoption of trade measures, 1971–1985

	Number of actions initiated by EC against all countries			*Number of actions initiated by EC against LDCs*		
Sector	*1971–5*	*1976–80*	*1981–5*	*1971–5*	*1976–80*	*1981–5*
Textiles and clothing	4	6	7	3 (2)*	3 (3)	4 (3)
Leather, footwear and travel goods	—	1	2	—	1 (1)	2 (1)
Wood and cork manufactures	—	4	5	—	3 (3)	2 (2)
Paper	—	4	4	—	1 (1)	2 (2)
Chemicals	1	11	30	1 (1)	—	10 (6)
Rubber manufactures	1	4	—	—	3 (3)	—
Iron and steel	1	19	15	1 (1)	14 (14)	10 (10)
Manufactures of metal	—	5	3	—	1 (1)	2 (2)
Transport equipment	—	1	3	—	1 (1)	2 (1)
Electrical machinery	—	6	6	—	2 (1)	1 (1)
Machinery (other than electrical)	—	2	—	—	—	—
Other products	—	7	22	—	4 (3)	12 (8)
Total	7	70	97	5 (4)	33 (31)	47 (36)

Table 6.1 Con't

	Number of actions initiated by USA against all countries			*Number of actions initiated by USA against LDCs*		
	1971–5	*1976–80*	*1981–5*	*1971–5*	*1976–80*	*1981–5*
Textiles and clothing	1	9	11	—	2 (1)	10 (4)
Leather, footwear and travel goods	1	8	—	1 (1)	7 (2)	—
Wood and cork manufactures	2	—	1	—	—	—
Paper	—	2	3	—	—	—
Chemicals	5	7	9	1 (1)	3 (1)	6 (2)
Rubber manufactures	1	2	1	—	2 (2)	—
Iron and steel	4	8	66	—	4 (3)	47 (35)
Manufactures of metal	2	1	7	—	—	1
Transport equipment	2	3	3	—	1 (1)	1 (1)
Electrical machinery	—	3	10	—	1 (1)	2 (2)
Machinery (other than electrical)	1	3	—	—	2 (1)	—
Other products	10	15	41	3 (3)	7 (5)	20 (13)
Total	29	61	152	5 (5)	29 (17)	87 (57)

* The figures in parentheses indicate the number of NTBs adopted against NICs. Antidumping and countervailing measures are included for both the EC and the USA. In addition, safeguard actions are included in the case of the EC and escape clauses in the case of the USA.

Source: *Official Journal of the European Community*, Brussels; Office of the US Trade Representative, *Trade Actions Monitoring System*, Washington, DC.

oriented growth strategies in the face of uncertain or diminishing market access (Helleiner 1981, Diaz-Alejandro and Helleiner 1982, 1987, Singer and Ansari 1988). According to this view, sooner or later there will be a "crowding out" of exports from less developed countries, either because of overproduction and declining profitability or a blocking protectionist response by industrial countries – or both. Finally, some analysts suggest that protectionism may fragment the framework of the General Agreement on Tariffs and Trade (GATT) by pushing developing countries further away from it (Frank 1981).

Empirical evidence on the actual impact of protectionism on developing country trade is limited. Analysis has been confined to export flows or market penetration ratios (Hughes and Waelbroeck 1981, Hughes and Krueger 1984, Cline 1984, Balassa and Balassa 1984, Hughes and Newbery 1986). These show that developing country exports of manufactures continued to grow in the 1970s and 1980s and to penetrate industrial country markets. The evidence on specific highly protected sectors such as textiles and apparel is slightly less uniform. Export flows to Europe seem to have slowed down considerably since the mid-1970s, while flows to the United States, after decelerating in the 1970s, resumed strong growth in the 1980s. On the whole, the quantitative controls set up under the MFAs seemed to have had the desired effect of slowing down developing country exports, but various leaks in the quota-based system put in place also became evident (Hamilton 1987, 1988, Wolf 1983, Cable 1987).

These empirical findings, however, go only as far as to indicate that protectionism in industrial countries did not totally inhibit export growth in developing countries. They do not mean that protectionism was harmless to developing countries in general or to the NICs in particular. To arrive at such a conclusion one would need to analyze the damage to developing countries, in terms of foregone growth, caused by protectionism in industrial countries, starting with the trade- and investment-inhibiting effects that import restrictions might have had in the countries against which they were taken. Even to evaluate the direct trade losses suffered by developing countries because of non-tariff protectionism, one needs a notion of what would have happened to developing country exports in the absence of protectionism. And this counterfactual evidence is simply not available, among other things, because the price-raising effects of many NTBs in use are not known, and not even all barriers to trade, especially the informal ones, are known with certainty.

In the absence of the most basic information on net export losses suffered by developing countries as a result of non-tariff trade restrictions, no strong conclusion should be drawn, on the basis of analysis of trade flows, on the effectiveness, or lack thereof, of the new protectionism. Its bite could conceivably have been very strong either in the aggregate or, as seems more plausible, in specific sectors. The only analysis of trade performance conducted for different functional categories of developing countries (Hughes and Newbery 1986) does point to the existence of differentiated effects, for example, between the first and second generation of newly industrializing developing countries.

A related question, which so far has not been fully investigated, is how developing countries have adjusted to the new protectionism. This chapter focuses on the trade responses of developing countries to the NTBs erected by industrial countries in the 1970s and 1980s. The analysis is based on the geographical and product patterns of developing country trade, and attempts to answer the question of how predictable, on the basis of neoclassical trade theory, these responses have been.

Trade responses of developing countries to increased protection in industrial countries

In a stylized three-region world where trade takes place only between developed countries, developing countries, and the remainder of the world, and a fair amount of product homogeneity is assumed to exist, if one starts from a position of free trade and goes to one of constrained trade between two of the regions (going to greater trade constraints does not change the picture), one would expect both trade creation and trade diversion effects to occur. Specifically postulating that trade protection increases only in industrial countries and affects only developing countries, one would expect that developing country exports to the rest of the world and the rest of the world's exports to industrial countries would go up, depending on the responsiveness of the relevant supplies and demands to the price variations caused by the changes in protection.

If, in addition, trade protection in industrial countries is selective in terms of products – one of the main characteristics of non-tariff protection – then one would also expect changes in the commodity composition of exports from the countries that are the targets of the restrictive trade measures. Developing countries, in other words, can be expected not only to switch geographical markets, from more protected ones to less protected ones, but also to switch products or export sectors from those specifically targeted by protection to those kept free from it.

Finally, if differences in the country targeted by the trade restrictions are taken into account, and developing countries are divided into two groups according to whether they are more or less targeted, one would expect the latter group to expand its exports to industrial countries at the expense of the former. Broadly speaking, the NECs can be expected to benefit from this type of trade deflection at the expense of the NICs.

Protectionism has other effects on trade flows that are disregarded here. One, which results from the lack of homogeneity in non-tariff practices, is an increase in intra-industrial country trade. Whenever industrial countries do not apply to each other the same export restrictions that they apply towards the rest of the world, exports from those industrial countries that are not the target of protection towards those that practice it vis-à-vis developing countries can, in fact, be expected to go up. Effects of this type are evident, for example, in the textiles sector. Under the MFAs, industrial countries restrict their individual imports from a number of developing countries, but do not at the same time restrict trade among themselves. Trade deflection, at the expense of developing countries whose exports are restricted by quotas, seems to have contributed in the last few years to industrial country imports from other industrial countries expanding more rapidly than imports from developing countries. This effect has been observed under many other VERs and has recently been studied in detail (Hamilton 1988).

There are aspects of the real world that this simple analysis ignores, such as the effects on labor and capital flows produced by protection. A preliminary review of the flows of private foreign investment to the NICs shows substantial declines from the mid-1970s to the mid-1980s. If this drop were related to trade protection, these changes in external (private) capital flows would constitute another important indication of the hidden, long-term impact of trade policy changes in the North.

Actual responses: changes in the geographical and product composition of exports of manufactures from developing countries

Throughout the 1970s, total developing country exports of manufactures expanded at the same pace as in the 1960s, that is, about 13 percent a year (table 6.2). This was remarkable considering the sharply reduced pace of economic activity in industrial countries, the extent of non-tariff protection, and the fairly widespread use in many developed countries of subsidies to restructure industrial sectors (such as steel, shipbuilding, synthetic fibers, and textiles).

Both demand and supply factors may have contributed to this outcome. On the demand side the slowdown in the growth of aggregate import demand in the industrial countries, which absorb more than 60 percent of developing country exports of manufactures, was possibly compensated by a reduction in tariff protection stemming from the Tokyo Round of trade

Table 6.2 Average annual percent change[a] in exports of manufactures[b] by main producing areas (constant 1980 dollars)[c]

Exporters	*1965–73*	*1983–80*	*1980–6*
Industrial countries[d]	10.5	5.1	3.4
Developing countries	12.9	12.6	9.1
NICs[e]	17.9	14.2	9.2
NECs[f]	14.3	14.3	14.7
India and China	2.3	9.3	8.4
Others[g]	8.6	5.3	−1.3
High-income oil exporters[h]	16.2	20.8	0.6
Total[i]	10.7	6.1	4.4

[a] Least squares growth rates.
[b] Manufactures are defined as SITC (REV1) 5 + 6 + 7 + 8 + 9 − 68.
[c] Values of exports deflated by indices of unit values of exports: (1) UN index of unit values of exports of manufactures for industrial countries; (2) UN indices of unit values of exports of manufactures for 37 developing countries (accounting for percent of total exports) and average of these indices for those developing countries for which national indices are not available; (3) 90 UN indices for three major high-income oil exporters and average of these three indices for the four other countries of this group.
[d] OECD countries, excluding Spain, Greece, Portugal, Yugoslavia, and Turkey.
[e] Korea, Taiwan, Hong Kong, Singapore, Mexico, Brazil, Yugoslavia, Greece, Spain, and Portugal (OECD definition).
[f] Turkey, Malaysia, Philippines, Israel, Morocco, Indonesia, Thailand, Bangladesh, Chile, Venezuela, and Peru.
[g] Other developing countries, excluding South Africa, NICs, and NECs.
[h] Libya, Saudi Arabia, Kuwait, United Arab Emirates, Baharain, Brunei and Qatar.
[i] Includes South Africa.
Sources: COMTRADE System; UN *Monthly Bulletin of Statistics*; UN Statistical Office.

negotiations, and tariff preferences for developing country exports of manufactures (except textiles and clothing) under the Generalized System of Preferences (GSPs).

On the supply side the capacity to export manufactures was expanding rapidly as a result of product diversification and a broadened industrial base in many developing countries. Nontraditional manufactures, (including machinery, transport equipment, chemicals, and nonmetallic mineral products) came to account for 60 percent of total shipments of manufactures, at the expense of exports of traditional labor-intensive, resource-based goods (such as textiles, apparel, pulp, paper, wood and metal products, and iron and steel). Several countries appeared poised to join the NICs as sizable exporters of manufactures, benefitting from export-oriented domestic policies and the globalization of industrial production. Moreover, their products became more price competitive, as relative factor abundances and learning-by-doing effects were more fully exploited.

In the 1980s the growth in the exports of manufactures from developing countries slowed to 9.1 percent a year, from the 12.6 percent a year of the previous decade (table 6.2). While still much faster than that of primary products (both oil and non-oil), the rate of growth of exports of manufactures seems to have suffered from the further slowdown in the pace of world economic activity that occurred in the 1980s, and the more restrictive trade policies that prevailed in industrial countries during the same years. During this period, while the tendency to use non-tariff protection against imports from developing countries picked up momentum, the countervailing effects of tariff reduction under the Tokyo Round and of extension of trade preferences under the GSPs waned.

None of the supply factors that helped sustain the growth of productive capacity and the price competitiveness of exports of developing countries in the 1970s appear to have subsided in the 1980s. If anything, the combined weight of debt in many middle-income developing countries and the demonstration effect of the successful NICs led to a greater reliance on exports of manufactures – and policy changes in this direction. For example, real devaluations became more numerous, more pronounced, and more sustained than in the 1970s.

An idea of the relative importance of demand and supply factors can be derived by comparing actual export performance in a given market in a certain period of time with expected performance at constant market shares. Between 1979 and 1986, for example, about 60 percent of the change in the value of exports of manufactures to industrial countries appears to be attributable to demand factors; the remainder to supply factors.[2]

To sustain the export drive, producers in developing countries seem to have first taken advantage of market opportunities in high-income oil exporting countries whose economies were booming in the 1970s[3] and whose markets remained at least as accessible as before. The rate of growth of exports of manufactures to these countries increased substantially in comparison to the 1960s, while the pace of exports to industrial countries slowed down considerably. In volume terms, exports to high-income oil exporting countries increased at 11.7 percent a year from 1973 to 1980, compared with 9.5 percent from 1965 to 1973, while growth in exports to industrial countries fell from 15.9 percent to 13.3 percent (table 6.3). The NICs in particular appear to have successfully diversified their export markets by doubling the growth of shipments of manufactured exports to high-income oil exporting countries in the 1970s. China and India also appear to have taken advantage of the opportunities offered by these markets, while deliveries from the NECs continued at the same rate as in the

Table 6.3 Average annual percent change in exports of manufactures from developing countries by main areas of destination (constant 1980 dollars)

	Areas of destination, 1963–73			*Areas of destination, 1973–80*			*Areas of destination, 1980–6*		
Exporters	*Industrial countries*	*Rest of world*	*Total*	*Industrial countries*	*Rest of world*	*Total*	*Industrial countries*	*Rest of world*	*Total*
Developing countries	15.9	9.5	12.9	13.3	11.7	12.6	11.6	4.5	9.1
NICs	23.3	9.9	17.9	12.1	18.2	14.2	11.4	5.5	9.2
NECs	14.8	13.7	14.3	14.6	13.9	14.3	15.1	13.8	14.7
India and China	2.5	2.2	2.3	11.5	8.0	9.3	10.2	7.2	8.4
Others	−2.3	17.0	8.6	23.4	−13.1	5.3	5.8	−12.9	−1.3

See notes to Table 6.2 for definitions of terms and categories of countries.
Source: COMTRADE System.

1960s. In the 1980s when oil prices collapsed, only the NECs continued to export manufactures at a substantially unchanged rate; the pace of export growth from the NICs, and to a lesser extent India and China slowed down (table 6.3).

In addition, developing countries successfully adapted the product composition of manufactured exports to changes in market conditions in industrial countries. Upgrading and product diversification are continuing phenomena. They have to do with trends in comparative advantage, diffusion of technology, and the product cycle. They are fostered by the role of multinational corporations in varying the location of production. Yet analysis of this phenomenon during the 1970s and 1980s shows two distinctive features. Not only did the tempo of diversification quicken, but changes in product composition of exports to industrial countries seemed to be closely related to the spread of non-tariff protection. Developing country exports moved from more protected to less protected sectors.

The share of traditional manufactures in the total exports of developing to industrial countries shows the largest relative decline from 1970 to 1986: 5.3 percent from 1970 to 1978, and another 6.8 percent between 1978 and 1986 (table 6.4). Within this group, the share of labor-intensive products declined most rapidly. These industrial sectors not only received the greatest amount of assistance from the advanced countries during the 1970s, but were also those in which non-tariff trade protection was strongest. From 1978 to 1986 the decline in the share of clothing exports and textiles was severe, while leather, footwear, and travel goods kept their market share. By most measurable standards – number of VERs in existence, frequency of other non-tariff measures applied against inputs and trade coverage of MFNs – these were the products most affected by the new protectionism of industrial countries. In contrast, the export market shares of developing countries in machinery and non-metallic mineral products surged, buoyed by a rise in demand and less stringent trade protection.

The successful diversification into electrical and nonelectrical machinery during this period, however, reflects the performance of only a few Asian NICs. The same is true for transport equipment. The four countries in question – Korea, Taiwan, Singapore, and Hong Kong – now account for about 70 percent of total developing country exports of machinery and transport products, up from 50 percent in 1975. Seemingly successful diversification can, therefore, hide profound changes in the sources of exports, indicating strong asymmetries in the benefits received by different groups of countries.

Finally, producers in developing countries made strong efforts to maintain the international competitiveness of their manufactured products, as shown by the increases in market shares that they attained (OECD 1986). While

Table 6.4 Changes in the product structure of manufactured exports from developing countries to industrial countries, 1970–86

Products (SITC)	Change in % share of exports[a] 1970–8	1978–86
Traditional Manufactures		
Labor-intensive		
Clothing (84)	+4.8	−4.1
Textiles (65)	−9.6	−3.2
Leather, footwear and travel goods (61 + 83 + 85)	+1.8	0
Total	−3.0	−7.3
Resource-based		
Rubber (62)	+0.1	+0.4
Wood and cork (63)	−2.2	−0.9
Paper (64)	+0.2	+0.4
Iron and steel (67)	−0.1	+0.1
Metals (69)	+0.6	+0.5
Total	−1.4	+0.5
Non-traditional Manufactures		
Electrical machinery (72)	+6.0	+4.7
Nonelectrical machinery (71)	+0.4	+4.8
Chemicals (5)	−6.0	−1.6
Transport equipment (73)	+1.5	+1.5
Nonmetallic minerals (66)	+3.4	−2.6
Total	+5.3	+6.8

[a] Computed from 1980 dollar values (current values deflated with indices of prices of various SITC categories of exported manufactures from a sample of developing countries). Miscellaneous manufactures were not included in the total.

Sources: *COMTRADE System* for value data, *National Sources* for the export prices of Korea, Taiwan, Hong Kong, Singapore, Yugoslavia, and Greece. *COMTRADE System* for the unit values of exports of Spain, Portugal, Mexico, and Brazil.

product quality and marketing improvements certainly played a part in the successful expansion of developing country market shares, price competitiveness seems to have been a major objective pursued by developing country exporters and a major factor in determining the success that they achieved. Prices of manufactures exported by developing countries fell 2

Table 6.5 Income and export price movements, 1965–86

	Average annual % change[a]		
	1965–73	*1973–80*	*1980–6*
Real GNP			
Industrial countries	4.5	2.8	2.5
High-income oil exporters	8.7	8.0	−3.5
Relative prices of manufactured exports			
Developing countries / Industrial countries	1.6	−2.2	−1.0
NICs / Industrial countries	1.7	−2.3	−0.4
NECs / Industrial countries	0.5	−0.5	−2.0
Terms of trade in developing countries	NA	−1.2	0.3[b]
NICs	NA	−1.1	−0.2[b]
NECs	NA	0.6	−3.8[b]

[a] Least squares growth rates.
[b] 1980–5 only.
Sources: OECD, *Main Economic Indicators*; IMF, *International Financial Statistics* (and Supplements); UN, *Monthly Bulletin of Statistics*; UNCTAD, *Handbook of International Trade and Development Statistics*; UN, Statistical Office.

percent a year from 1973 to 1980, relative to those of industrial countries, after having increased at almost the same rate from the mid-1960s to the early 1970s. The decline continued in the 1980s, albeit at a slower pace, namely, 1 percent a year (table 6.5). Implicit in the cumulative declines that occurred in relative prices are sizable gains in demand. Given the available evidence on the values of the price elasticities of world import demand (Faini, Clavijo, and Senhadji 1988), an average yearly decline in relative export prices of 1.5 percent means a yearly increase in import demand of about 2.5 to 3 percent, other things being equal.

From 1973 to 1986, export trends varied substantially among developing countries. The NICs were overtaken in terms of growth of exports of manufactures by the NECs. Exports from this group expanded at almost exactly the same rate that had been attained by the NICs between 1973 and 1980 (about 14 percent a year), and continued into the 1980s, at which time the growth of exports from the NICs slowed to about 9 percent (table 6.2). These trend differences can be attributed in part to the fact that the NECs were less burdened by protection, and in part to more competitive pricing. In fact, from 1980 to 1986 the prices of manufactures from the NECs declined faster than those of the NICs – an annual 2 percent compared to 0.4 percent – and NEC export shipments, in terms of growth, outperformed, those of the NICs in both industrial countries and in the rest of the world (table 6.5). These trends in relative export prices appear to support the hypothesis of export competition among developing countries and thus the conclusion that some "adding-up" constraints may indeed be at work.

Exports of manufactures from China expanded during the 1970s and the 1980s, albeit from relatively small bases. Exports from India picked up momentum in the 1980s. Changes in domestic policies were instrumental in reviving export growth in these two large and traditionally closed economies whose combined export growth in the 1980s paralleled that of the NICs (table 6.5). But the export performance of the rest of the developing countries worsened considerably in the 1980s, when exports of manufactures contracted. The collapse of demand in high-income oil exporting countries seems to have been the main cause of the decline (table 6.3).

Conclusion

In the aggregate, developing countries seem to have adapted quite successfully to the fallout from weak demand and limited market access in the industrial countries. Exports of manufactures moved up at a fast rate overall, even if some appreciable decline has become apparent in recent years.

In the 1970s, developing exporters followed a strategy of shifting exports from industrial country markets to those of high-income oil exporting countries in accord with the expectations that can be derived from a three-region model of the world, such as the one set out in this chapter, in which trade protection is specifically directed against only one of the regions. In the 1980s, when market diversion possibilities diminished because of a slowdown in demand in the previously booming oil exporting region, and trade protection reduced shipments to industrial countries, the rate of expansion of developing country exports of manufactures declined appreciably in both markets as well as in the aggregate.

Developing countries also reacted to the product-specific non-tariff protectionism practiced by industrial countries by diverting productive resources from heavily protected into less protected industries. This has resulted in a cut in the export share of traditional manufactures and an increase in the share of nontraditional products. This product upgrading, however, was largely limited to the four Asian NICs.

Significant differences in overall export performance became evident in the period under review. The second generation of exporters of manufactures reached and surpassed the first generation. Considering that (1) the manufacturing industries of the NICs were the major targets of non-tariff barriers; (2) supply incentives remained strong in both the NICs and the NECs; and (3) the two sets of countries faced roughly similar demand conditions the relatively faster growth in exports of the NECs from 1973 to 1986 seems to be consistent with expectations regarding the intercountry effects of non-tariff protectionism. The NECs, in other words, appear to have taken advantage of the barriers erected against the NICs. During the 1980s, moreover, the NECs seem also to have provided the NICs with strong price competition in export markets.

China (and to a lesser extent India) appears to have filled whatever residual export opportunity for manufactures became available during this period, including any vacuum in product- and country-specific trade restrictions. An additional consideration is that these large developing countries are more capable of negotiating successfully at the political and the economic level with industrial country governments and thus stand a better chance of containing restrictions against their exports. No other significant group of developing countries appear to have shared in the growth of manufactured exports.

This analysis of trade flows in the 1970s and 1980s does not provide any direct and clear-cut answer to the question of how binding for developing countries was the new trade protectionism practiced by industrial countries. It does, nonetheless, suggest that trade protectionism was not a marginal factor for developing countries. Observed changes in the geographical destination and product composition of manufactured exports, as well as intra-developing-country export flows, are largely consistent with the hypothesis of efficacy of the non-tariff barriers to trade used by industrial countries against developing countries.

Notes

* The views expressed in this chapter are those of the author. They should not in any way be attributed to the organizations with which he is affiliated.

1 Some of the key restrictions affecting footwear exports have since been lifted.
2 Between 1979 and 1986 exports of manufactures from developing countries to IECD countries increased by $77.6 billion. The hypothetical increase in constant 1979 market share would have been $46.7 billion, leaving a difference of $30.9 billion.
3 See table 6.5 for details of income growth.

References

Anderson, K., and R. Baldwin. 1981. The political market for protection in industrial countries, World Bank Staff Working Paper no. 492, Washington, DC.

Anderson, K., and R. Garnaut. 1987. *Australian Protectionism: Extent, Causes and Effects*, Allen and Unwin, Sidney.

Anjaria, S. J., Z. Iqbal, L. L. Perez, and W. S. Tseng. 1981. Trade policy developments in industrial countries, International Monetary Fund Occasional Paper no. 5, Washington, DC.

Balassa, B. 1971. Trade policies in developing countries, *American Economic Review, Papers and Proceedings*, 61: 178–87.

Balassa, B. 1978a. Export incentives and export performance in developing countries: a comparative analysis, *Weltwirtschaftliches Archiv*, 114: 24–60.

Balassa, B. 1978b. Exports and economic growth: further evidence, *Journal of Development Economics*, 5: 181–9.

Balassa, B. 1981. *The Newly Industrializing Developing Countries in the World Economy*, Pergamon, New York.

Balassa, B. 1984. Trade between developed and developing countries: the decade ahead, *OECD Economic Studies*, 3: 7–25.

Balassa, B. 1985. Exports, policy choices and economic growth in developing countries after the 1973 oil shock, *Journal of Development Economics*, 18: 23–35.

Balassa, B. 1988. The adding up problem, World Bank Policy Planning and Research Working Paper, Washington, DC.

Balassa, B., and C. Balassa. 1984. Industrial protection in developed countries, *The World Economy*, 7: 179–96.

Baldwin, R. 1982. The inefficacy of trade policy, Princeton Essay in International Finance no. 150, Princeton, NJ.

Baldwin, R. 1985a. *The Political Economy of US Import Policy*, MIT Press, Cambridge, MA.

Baldwin, R. 1985b. The inefficacy of protection in promoting social goals, *The World Economy*, 8: 109–18.

Bhagwati, J. 1987. Outward orientation: trade issues, in V. Corbo, M. Goldstein, and M. Khan (eds), *Growth Oriented Adjustment Programs*, International Monetary Fund and The World Bank, Washington, DC.

Bhagwati, J. 1988. *Protectionism*, MIT Press, Cambridge, MA.

Bhagwati, J., and T. N. Srinivasan. 1978. Trade policy and development in R. Dornbusch and J. Frenkel (eds), *International Economic Policy: Theory and Evidence*, Johns Hopkins University Press, Baltimore, MD.

Boonekamp, C. F. 1987. Voluntary export restraints, *Finance and Development*, 4: 2–5.

Cable, V. 1987. Textiles and clothing in a new round of trade negotiations, *The World Bank Economic Review*, 1: 549–69.

Cable, V., and I. Rebelo. 1980. Britain's pattern of specialization in manufactured goods with developing countries and trade protection, World Bank Staff Working Paper no. 425, Washington, DC.

Caves, R. E. 1976. Models of political choice: Canada's tariff structure, *Canadian Journal of Economics*, 9: 278–300.

Cline, W. 1982. Can the East Asian model of development be generalized, *World Development*, February: 71–90.

Cline, W. 1984. *Exports of Manufactures from Developing Countries*, The Brookings Institution, Washington, DC.

Diaz-Alejandro, C. 1975. Trade policies and economic development, in P. B. Kennen (ed.), *International Trade and Finance: Frontiers for Research*, Cambridge University Press, Cambridge.

Diaz-Alejandro, C., and G. Helleiner. 1982. *Handmaiden in Distress: World Trade in the 1980s*, Overseas Development Council, Washington, DC.

Diaz-Alejandro, C., and G. Helleiner, 1987. Developing countries and the reform of the world trading system, in D. Salvatore (ed.), *The New Protectionist Threat to World Welfare*, North Holland, New York.

Faini, R., F. Clavijo, and A. Senhadji. 1988. International demand constraints to export growth in LDCs, The World Bank's Country Economics Department (processed), Washington, DC.

Feder, G. 1982. On exports and economic growth, *Journal of Development Economics*, 12: 59–73.

Finger, J. M., H. K. Hall, and D. R. Nelson. 1982. The political economy of administered protection, *American Economic Review*, 72: 452–66.

Finger, J. M., and A. Olechowski (eds). 1987. *The Uruguay Round: A Handbook on the Multilateral Trade Negotiations*, The World Bank, Washington, DC.

Frank, I. 1981. Trade policy issues for the developing countries, World Bank Staff Working Paper no. 478, Washington, DC.

Gard, L., and J. Riedel. 1980. Safeguard protection of industry in developed countries: assessment of the implications for developing countries, *Weltwirtschaftliches Archiv*, 116: 471–92.

Glismann, H. H., and F. D. Weiss. 1980. On the political economy of protection in Germany, World Bank Staff Working Paper no. 427, Washington, DC.

Grilli, E. R. 1988a. Contemporary protectionism in an unstable world economy, in G. Sutija and G. Phels (eds) *Protectionism and International Banking*, MacMillan, London (forthcoming).

Grilli, E. R. 1988b. The macroeconomic determinants of trade protection in the 1970s and 1980s, *The World Economy*, 11: 313–26.

Grilli, E. R., and M. La Noce. 1983. The political economy of protection in Italy: some empirical evidence, *Banca Nazionale del Lavoro Quarterly Review*, 145: 143–61.

Hamilton, C. B. 1987. *The New Protectionism with Special Reference to Europe*, World Development Report Background Paper, The World Bank, Washington, DC (processed).

Hamilton, C. B. 1988. Restrictiveness and international transmission of the new protectionism, in R. E. Baldwin, C. B. Hamilton, and A. Sapir (eds), *Issues in US–EC Trade Relations*, University of Chicago Press, Chicago.

Havrylyshyn, O., and I. Alikhani. 1982. Is there cause for export optimism: an inquiry into the existence of a second generation of successful exporters, *Weltwirtschaftliches Archiv*, 4: 651–62.

Havrylyshyn, O., and M. Wolf. 1983. Recent trends in trade among developing countries, *European Economic Review*, 21: 333–62.

Helleiner, G. K. 1981. *International Economic Disorder: Essays in North–South Relations*, University of Toronto Press, Toronto.

Helleiner, G. K. 1986. Outward orientation, import instability, and African economic growth: an empirical investigation, in S. Lall and F. Stewart (eds), *Theory and Reality in Development: Essays in Honor of Paul Streeten*, St. Martin's Press, New York.

Heller, P., and R. C. Porter. 1978. Export and growth: an empirical reinvestigation, *Journal of Economic Development*, 5: 191–3.

Hughes, H., and Waelbroeck. 1981. Can developing country exports keep growing in the 1980s, *The World Economy*, 4: 127–47.

Hughes, H., and A. O. Krueger. 1984. "Effects of protection in developed countries on developing countries' exports of manufactures," in R. E. Baldwin and A. O. Krueger (eds), *The Structure and Evolution of Recent US Trade Policy*, University of Chicago Press, Chicago.

Hughes, G. A., and D. M. G. Newbery. 1986. Protection and developing countries' exports of manufactures, *Economic Policy*, 2: 410–53.

Jung, S. W., and P. J. Marshall. 1985. Export, growth and causality in developing countries, *Journal of Development Economics*, 18: 1–12.

Kavoussi, R. 1984. Exports and economic growth: further empirical evidence, *Journal of Development Economics*, 14: 241–50.

Kavoussi, R. 1985. International trade and economic development: recent experience of developing countries, *Journal of Developing Areas*, 19: 379–92.

Koekkoek, K. A., J. Kol, and L. B. M. Mennes. 1981. On protectionism in the Netherlands, World Bank Staff Working Paper no. 493, Washington, DC.

Kostecki, M. 1987. Export restraint arrangements and trade liberalization, *The World Economy*, 10: 425–53.

Krueger, A. O. 1978. *Liberalization Attempts and Consequences*, Ballinger, Cambridge, MA.

Krueger, A. O. 1980. Trade policies as an input for development, *American Economic Review, Papers and Proceedings*, 70: 288–92.

Krueger, A. O. 1983. *Trade and Employment in Developing Countries: Synthesis and Conclusions*, University of Chicago Press, Chicago.

Krueger, A. O. 1984. Trade policies in developing countries in R. W. Jones and P. B. Kennen (eds), *Handbook of International Economics*, vol. 1, Elsevier Science Publishers, New York.

Lewis, W. A. 1980. The slowing down of the engine of growth, *American Economic Review*, 70: 555–64.

Michaely, M. 1977. Exports and growth: an empirical investigation, *Journal of Development Economics*, 4: 49–53.

Nishimizu, M., and S. Robinson. 1984. Trade policies and productivity changes in developing countries, *Journal of Development Economics*, 16: 177–206.

Nogues, J., A. Olechowski, and A. Winters. 1986. The extent of non-tariff barriers to industrial countries' imports, *The World Bank Economic Review*, 1: 181–99.

Nowzad, B. 1978. *The Rise in Protectionism*, International Monetary Fund Pamphlet Series, no. 8, Washington, DC.

Olechowski, A., and G. Sampson. 1980. Current trade restrictions in the EEC, the United States and Japan, *Journal of World Trade Law*, 3: 220–31.

Organization for Economic Cooperation and Development. 1986. The OECD Compatible Trade and Production Data Base: 1970–83, Department of Economics and Statistics Working Paper no. 31, Paris.

Pincus, J. J. 1975. Pressure groups and the patterns of tariffs, *Journal of Political Economy*, 83: 757–78.

Prebish, R. 1983. The crisis of capitalism and international trade, *CEPAL Review*, 20: 51–74.

Ram, R. 1985. Exports and economic growth: some additional evidence, *Economic Development and Cultural Change*, 3: 415–25.

Ray, E. J. 1981. The determinants of tariff and non-tariff trade restrictions in the United States, *Journal of Political Economy*, 89: 105–21.

Ray, E. J., and H. P. Marvel. 1984, The pattern of protection in the industrialized world, *The Review of Economics and Statistics*, 66: 452–8.

Riedel, J. 1984. Trade as the engine of growth in developing countries, revisited, *The Economic Journal*, 94: 56–73.

Salvatore, D. 1987. Import penetration, exchange rates and protectionism in the United States, *Journal of Policy Modeling*, 9: 125–41.

Singer, H. W., and J. A. Ansari. 1988. *Rich and Poor Countries*, Unwin Hyman, London.

Singer, H. W., and P. Gray. 1988. Trade policy and growth of developing countries: some new data, *World Development*, 16: 395–403.

Streeten, P. 1982. A cool look at outward-looking strategies for development, *The World Economy*, 5: 159–69.

Takacs, W. 1981. Pressures for protectionism: an empirical analysis, *Economic Inquiry*, 19: 687–93.

Taylor, L. 1982. Back to basics: theory and rhetoric in the North–South round, *World Development*, 10: 327–35.

Tharakan, P. K. M. 1980. The political economy of protection in Belgium, World Bank Staff Working Paper no. 431, Washington, DC.

Tyler, W. 1981. Growth and export expansion in developing countries, *Journal of Development Economics*, 9: 121–30.

Wolf, M. 1983. Managed trade: implications of the textile arrangements, in W. R. Cline (ed.), *Trade Policy in the 1980s*, Institute for International Economics, Washington, DC.

7

The State of Debate on Trade and Industrialization in Developing Countries

James Riedel

For over two decades a great debate was waged between the proponents of the inward-oriented and the outward-oriented industrialization strategies. Although no formal armistice has been signed, and skirmishes continue to break out, one side in this debate can claim a clear and decisive victory. At the end of a successful campaign it is rewarding to look back and be reminded of how victory was won. I will indulge in some of that, reviewing briefly the theoretical and empirical arguments used to demonstrate the superiority of what has become known as the export promotion (EP) strategy over its arch-rival the import substitution (IS) strategy. But that is not the main purpose of this chapter, since it has already been done by many of those who led the battle (Bhagwati, 1987, 1988; Krueger, 1984; Little, 1982; Lal, 1983; and Lal and Rajapatirana, 1987; Srinivasan, 1986a). Instead, the chapter's main purpose is to explain what victory for the EP strategy means: what issues were won, what issues were conceded, and what issues are still being contested. Do the on-going skirmishes over as yet unresolved issues pose a threat to the hegemonic position the EP strategy currently enjoys within the economics profession, if not among policymakers in developing countries?

What victory means

The ascendancy of the EP strategy was a victory for "markets over mandarins", to use Deepak Lal's (1988) vivid phrase, but only to a limited extent. The case for EP does not argue for *laissez-faire*, or even for free trade. It does not even rule out IS, which most of the leading proponents of EP,

** Export subsidies

including Bhagwati, Balassa and Krueger, concede is an appropriate strategy in the early phase of industrialization and, if practiced selectively, is not precluded in later stages of industrialization when EP becomes the appropriate strategy.

What is required of an EP strategy, according to Bhagwati (1988), is simply the equality of the *average* effective exchange rate for exports (EER_X) and the *average* effective exchange rate for imports (EER_M). This is what Bhagwati calls "the trade-neutral or bias-free strategy". In contrast, the IS strategy is defined by a system of incentives in which $EER_X < EER_M$, while $EER_X > EER_M$ is termed the "ultra-export promotion" (UEP) strategy.

It is important to recognize that the EP strategy, as defined, is consistent with a substantial amount of policy-induced price distortion within the framework of an articulated program of *selective* IS. As Bhagwati (1988, p. 93) argues,

> We also need to remember always that the average EER_X and EER_M can and do conceal very substantial variations among different exports and among different imports... Thus, within the broad aggregates of an EP country case, there may well be activities that are being import substituted (i.e., their EER_M exceeds the average EER_X). Indeed, there often are.

Given that the EP strategy is consistent with substantial policy-induced price distortion, the notion that it is necessarily "trade-neutral or bias-free" is valid only in a limited sense. If, within a neutral trade regime, policy-induced distortions reduce the set of production possibilities, for example by introducing intersectoral differences in marginal factor productivities or by causing a diversion of resources to rent-seeking or other "directly unproductive" activities, there may remain a substantial bias against exports, either in terms of the absolute level of export production or in terms of the export sector's relative claim on resources.

The point is illustrated in figure 7.1, which is an adaptation of the diagram Bhagwati (1988) uses to distinguish between the IS, EP, and UEP strategies. The condition that the *average* EER_X should equal the *average* EER_M is equivalent to the condition that the average domestic opportunity cost of producing exports, in terms of foregone production of import-competing goods, should equal the average relative price of exports to import-competing goods in world markets, which in figure 7.1 is shown by tan θ. This condition is satisfied at point Y on AB, which, let us assume, is the frontier of a distortion-ridden production possibility set. The same condition holds at Y' on $A'B'$, which represents the frontier of a distortion-free production possibility set. The EP equilibrium at Y is clearly superior to either the IS equilibrium at X or the UEP equilibrium at Z; however, it cannot be

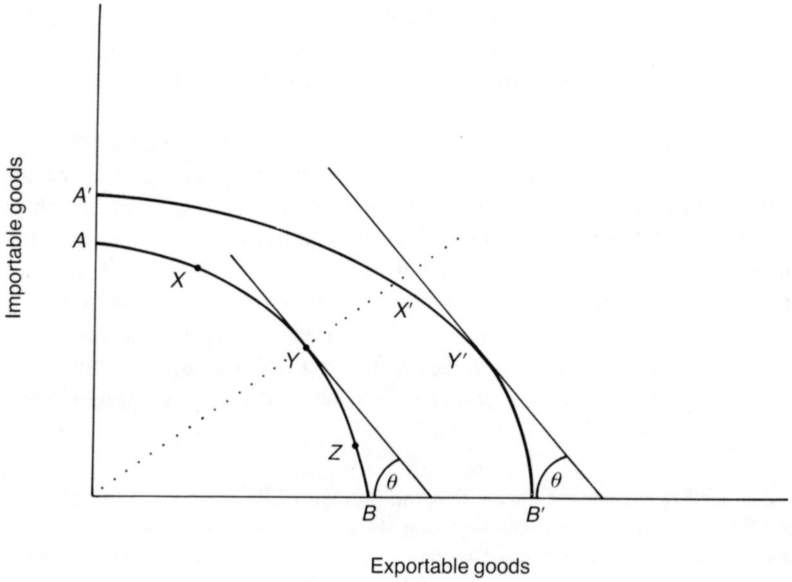

Figure 7.1

considered "trade-neutral or bias-free" over all possible outcomes, but only relative to alternative outcomes for a given set of production possibilities. Indeed, an IS policy whose only instrument was the exchange rate or, equivalently, a uniform tariff cum export tax, creating thereby a divergence between a *uniform* EER_M and a *uniform* EER_X (e.g. *X'* on *A'B'*), could be associated with a greater level of exports and a larger share of domestic output than would obtain under an EP regime in which there was substantial price distortion (e.g. *Y* on *AB*).

Why not free trade?

Why does the EP strategy recommend only that $EER_X = EER_M$ *on average* and not that EERs be uniform across all export and import-competing sectors? In other words, why a neutral trade regime but not necessarily a liberal or free trade regime?

Economic theory is not very generous in providing exceptions to the case for free trade. According to the conventional theory of trade, restrictions on trade are no better than second-best policy instruments, except in circumstances where a country can influence world prices of the goods it either exports or imports. However, when domestic markets are imperfect, because of externalities or other imperfections, restrictions on trade may be superior to free trade; in other words, a second-best trade policy may (or may not) be better than no trade policy at all.

It is on this fragile foundation that the oldest and most enduring argument for protection in developing countries, the infant industry argument, rests. The case for infant industry protection requires a series of conditions: first, that there are "economies of time" which make new firms or industries in LDCs uncompetitive with established foreign firms or industries; second, that it is not profitable for firms to enter an infant industry under free trade conditions, either because the long-run benefits are external to the firms or because the short-run losses cannot be financed against long-run profits; third, that if protected from foreign competition, domestic firms in infant industries will eventually be profitable under free trade conditions; fourth, that the short-term social opportunity costs of protecting an infant industry are outweighed by the long-term social benefits of having the industry established; and finally, that measures superior to trade policy are not available to promote infant industries.

Before examining whether the practice of infant industry protection in developing countries generally meets these conditions, it is useful to consider whether the so-called "new theory of trade," which emphasizes the implications of scale economies, imperfect competition, and product differentiation, offers any convincing arguments for protection.

Perhaps the most interesting and controversial proposal to be derived from the new trade theory is the idea of using trade restrictions to give domestic firms a strategic advantage in world markets. A role for strategic trade policy à la Brander and Spencer requires at a minimum that domestic firms in developing countries have the potential to establish a substantial position in world markets and that LDC governments can make a credible impression on foreign competitors by announcing trade policy initiatives (Krugman, 1986). Since there are few firms in LDCs with a commanding presence in world markets and few governments that are sufficiently well financed to make an aggressive strategic trade policy credible to foreign competitors, the potential for this kind of policy would seem to be extremely limited for developing countries.

There are, however, other applications of the new theory that may be more relevant. One is where oligopolistic foreign firms use their market power in small LDCs to extract rent. Srinivasan (1986b) shows how an optimal lump sum tax on the foreign firm combined with an optimal import subsidy can capture the oligopolist's rent for the host country. He concludes, however, that "while the logic of this argument is impeccable, whether many developing countries are capable of designing or credibly implementing such a two-part tariff is open to doubt" (p. 19).

Another recent argument for restricting trade is the idea of import protection as export promotion, a version of the old infant industry argument, but one which supposedly avoids the pitfalls of the original. It is suggested that protecting infant export industries is superior to protecting infant import-competing industries because export activities stimulate greater efficiency and productivity growth through direct competition in foreign markets and because expanding market opportunities abroad allow scale economies to be realized more quickly, reducing the cost and shortening the duration of infant industry protection (Westphal, 1982; Pack and Westphal, 1986). Srinivasan (1986b, p. 19) remains skeptical, however, arguing that "except perhaps for a few large developing economies that are at the same time sufficiently advanced technologically, developing countries by and large are unlikely to have domestic markets for high technology products, large enough for this argument for protection to be of any significance." Thus, Srinivasan concludes, "the exercise of an interventionist trade policy by developing countries, based on recent theories of oligopolistic competition and increasing returns, is unlikely to be beneficial." These sentiments are echoed by Krugman (1986) who argues that "there is nothing in the theory so far that would restore intellectual respectability to the strategy of import substitution. Import substituting industrialization looks even worse in the new theory than it does in the standard theory."

The evidence on infant industry protection

While IS may have lost intellectual respectability as a strategy, it still does have its advocates when it is applied selectively. Moreover, the theoretical justification for selective IS rests, as did the case for IS as a strategy, on one version or another of the old infant industry argument. And yet, Krueger and Tuncer (1982, p. 1142) claim that "there has been virtually no systematic examination of the empirical relevance of the infant industry argument". As they correctly argue:

> Even if there are conditions under which dynamic factors and externalities in an infant industry might warrant intervention, that does not prove that those conditions are in fact met. In the last analysis, defense of infant industry protection must rest on empirical grounds: do the long-run benefits justify the short-run costs of starting up an initially high-cost infant?

What evidence is there? Certainly there is ample evidence that beyond some point, IS as a strategy encounters rapidly diminishing returns, and that trade policy reforms which neutralize the disincentive to export, though not necessarily eliminate all trade restrictions, improve economic performance. This evidence is in fact the heart of the case for the EP strategy (which will be reviewed in the next section). It does not, however, provide much basis for judging the validity of the infant industry argument. The failure of the IS strategy as it has been practiced, spreading the net of protection ever wider, from consumer goods to intermediates and eventually to heavy capital-intensive investment goods industries, cannot easily be interpreted as a refutation of the underlying premises of the infant industry argument since such an all-encompassing system of protection is essentially inconsistent with the infant industry argument. It is inconsistent because one sector can be favored only at the expense of other sectors. To protect all is to protect none and thus to deny support to worthy infants which may deserve it.

If failure of the IS strategy is only a qualified indictment of the infant industry argument, what conclusions can be drawn from the relative success of the EP strategy? Ironically, the argument is commonplace that the EP strategy has been successful only because infant industry protection provided an industrial foundation on which it could build. This claim is, however, virtually impossible to substantiate, or refute, since every country save one, Hong Kong, started off with the IS strategy. Whether the EP strategy succeeded in East Asia and elsewhere because of, or inspite of, the earlier experience with the IS strategy is a moot issue, at least as far as those countries are concerned. However, since there are some countries, mainly in Africa, which may not yet have completed the "easy phase" of IS, the issue is not entirely moot. It may be asked whether such countries are ripe yet for the EP strategy, or whether they should press on with the IS strategy until such time as they achieve a level of industrialization comparable to that which Taiwan and South Korea had achieved when they first launched the EP strategy.

If the success or failure of the IS strategy is not a fair test of the infant industry argument, what is? Krueger and Tuncer (1982, p. 1143) suggest the following:

> the important aspect of the infant industry case seems summarizable in the proposition that, in order for it to be empirically valid, a necessary (but not sufficient) condition is that costs in (temporarily) assisted or protected industries should have fallen over time more rapidly than cost in nonprotected or less protected industries.

There are two reasons why one industry's unit costs could change relative to another's: either unit input requirements fall more (or rise less) than the other's, or the relative reward to the factor it uses relatively intensively falls. Krueger and Tuncer dismiss the latter as irrelevant to the infant industry argument, and focus on the former: "Should industry i have been protected on infant industry grounds and its costs have fallen relative to k, it will be judged that there were some dynamic factors in industry i that *may* have warranted intervention (although there is no presumption whatsoever that intervention was optimal)".

What Krueger and Tuncer find in the case of Turkey in the 1960s and 1970s, a country as committed as any to import substitution, is that there was no systematic tendency for more protected firms or industries to have had higher total factor productivity growth than less protected firms and industries. This, they suggest, is sufficient to prove that protection was not warranted.

Aside from the study by Krueger and Tuncer, there is scant evidence relating directly to the infant industry argument. In a recent paper Howard Pack (1986), a leading advocate of selective infant industry protection, surveyed the literature thoroughly and found little evidence of a difference in total factor productivity growth between relatively open and closed developing countries. The more rapid GDP (Gross Domestic Product) growth observed in more open economies must therefore be attributable to more rapid growth of resource endowment. Pack and Westphal (1986) imply that the lack of any significant difference in total factor productivity growth is a shortcoming of the EP strategy and undermines the validity of the underlying neo-classical theory. But of course it is the infant industry argument rather than any known theorem of neo-classical theory which suggests differences in productivity growth among sectors. Since the link between infant industry protection and intersectoral productivity growth differentials has yet to be established empirically, the argument remains, after all these years, a theoretical possibility without much to substantiate it.

The case for the export promotion strategy

Since so little empirical support can be found for the infant industry argument, one might reasonably ask why conventional wisdom stops short at a neutral trade regime rather than going all out for a free and neutral trade strategy in developing countries. The answer is simple. The case for the EP strategy was built on real world experience, rather than on pure theoretical reasoning. That is why the case is so powerful and appealing, even to "practical men" who, as Keynes noted, "believe themselves to be quite exempt from intellectual influences". Taiwan, South Korea and thereafter a number of countries showed that removing some, but not necessarily all, trade restrictions (especially the quantitative variety) and offsetting the bias against exports inherent in the IS regime, led almost invariably to improved economic performance. Bhagwati and others documented and painstakingly analyzed the successes and failures under the competing strategies and then, like good economists everywhere, set about to answer the question: "does what works in practice also work in theory?"

A free trade strategy works best of all in theory, but alas has rarely been tried in practice. The single case of it in recent times, Hong Kong, is a phenomenal success, but is routinely dismissed as irrelevant because of the peculiarities of Hong Kong (not the least of which is success itself). The case for the EP strategy is therefore a practical compromise between a free trade strategy, which looks good in theory but has not been practiced, and the IS strategy, which looks bad in theory and worse in practice.

The gains from (partial) trade liberalization, which is what implementation of the EP strategy requires, are well documented. There are two kinds of studies which purport to show the superiority of the EP strategy: country case studies of industrialization under different trade policy regimes (Little, Scitovsky, and Scott, 1970; Balassa, 1971; Donges and Riedel, 1976; Bhagwati, 1978; Krueger, 1978), and cross-country studies of the relationship between export expansion and economic growth (Michalopoulos and Jay, 1973; Michaely, 1977; Krueger, 1978; Balassa, 1978; Tyler, 1981;

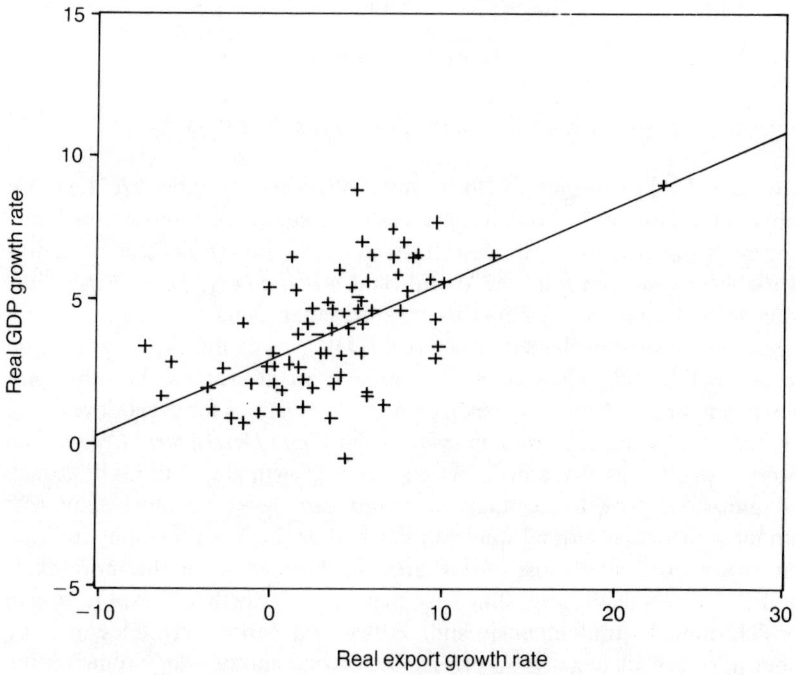

Figure 7.2 Real GDP and export growth rates (%), 1965–86

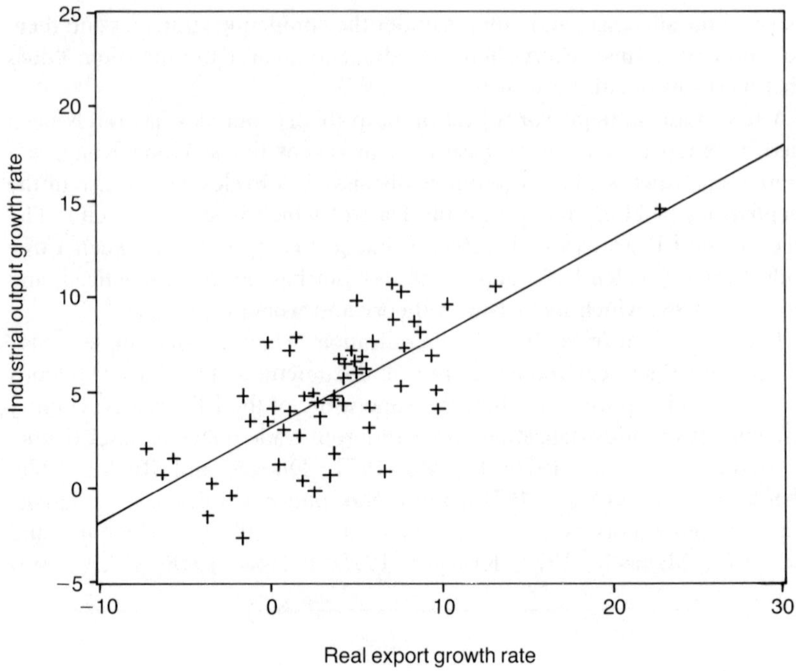

Figure 7.3 Industrial output and export growth rates (%), 1965–86

Feder, 1983). The former, as Bhagwati (1988) correctly notes, are the more compelling. The latter, however, are easier to summarize and better highlight the stylized facts of the case. Indeed, since the cross-country studies invariably rely on data from the World Bank's *World Development Report*, it is easier to replicate their results than to summarize them.

The simple relationships between real GDP growth and export growth on the one hand, and industrial growth and export growth on the other, are shown in figures 7.2 and 7.3, which contain observations for every developing country for which there are data in the *1988 World Development Report*. The observed positive associations between export growth and both GDP growth and industrial growth are suggestive, but can never be more than that without a theory. A primal question is whether these associations indicate that export expansion causes GDP growth, the reverse, or the more likely and more theoretically appealing case that output growth and export growth are determined simultaneously and, as two endogenous variables, may be either positively or negatively correlated with one another depending on the sources of economic change in the system.

There is, however, some evidence to suggest that export growth, standing as a proxy for openness, or as a force in its own right, exerts an independent positive influence on real output growth. That is, after the effects of capital accumulation and labor force growth are accounted for, export growth is found to have a strong and statistically significant positive effect on GDP growth (Balassa, 1978; Feder, 1983). This result is easily replicated using *World Development Report* data for all developing countries for which there are data ($\bar{R}^2 = 0.61$, $n = 75$, t-statistics given in parentheses):

$$\begin{aligned}\hat{Y} = &-1.20 &+ 0.13(I/Y) &+ 0.81\hat{L} &+ 0.22\hat{X}\\ &(-1.80) &(4.63) &(3.81) &(6.52)\end{aligned}$$

where $\hat{Y}$ is real GDP growth, I/Y is the average ratio of gross domestic investment to GDP, $\hat{L}$ is the labor force growth rate and $\hat{X}$ is the real export growth rate, all defined for the period 1965–86.

Numerous hypotheses have been offered to explain the strong independent influence of exports on GDP growth: improvement in allocative efficiency due to trade policy reform; demonstration effects from contact with foreign competitors; increased domestic competition; realization of scale economies; reduction in rent-seeking and "directly unproductive" activities; and various forms of X-efficiency gains. None of these effects is easy to identify empirically, but the weight of evidence, albeit some of it circumstantial, in favor of an outward-oriented or trade-neutral regime is undeniable.

And yet, many countries strenuously resist trade liberalization, often undertaking it only as a last resort during periods of economic crisis. It cannot be denied that liberalization has worked in the past, but there are many who doubt that it can work in the future. Among the concerns, the most prominent are:

1 that external demand for LDC exports is insufficient to justify an EP strategy;
2 that past successes of the EP strategy, especially in East Asia, were due to non-economic conditions which are absent and cannot be replicated elsewhere; and
3 that in many countries short-term macroeconomic stabilization goals preclude trade liberalization, at least for the foreseeable future.

The external demand constraint

Of all the excuses for erecting trade barriers, or not lowering them, export demand pessimism is by far the favorite. In the 1950s, when intellectual justification was sought for the IS strategy that most developing countries had already adopted, export demand pessimism was called into service by many of the pioneers of development economics, including Nurkse, Prebish, Myrdal and Chenery. Two decades later, in laying out the argument for a development strategy of collective self-reliance through the substitution of South–South trade for North–South trade, W. A. Lewis (1980) again called up export demand pessimism to provide justification. More recently, economists at the International Food Policy Research Institute have advocated an "agriculture-based development strategy", and not surprisingly they justify their otherwise sensible recommendations on grounds of weak demand for LDC manufactured exports (Bautista, 1988).

There are two sources of pessimism about demand for LDC exports of manufactures: (1) price inelastic demand and (2) protectionism in developed countries. The fact is that most econometric estimates of LDC export demand functions do indicate price inelasticity. The thorough review of the literature, by Goldstein and Khan (1985), found a "consensus view" that the price elasticity of demand for LDC exports (either in aggregate or for individual countries or commodity groups) is in the range of −0.5 to −1.0, with the income elasticity of demand between 2.0 and 4.0.

The problem with these estimates is that often they are not consistent with the way LDC exports behave. For example, following trade liberalization, some countries (e.g. Sri Lanka in the late 1970s and Turkey in the early 1980s) have experienced export growth rates as high as 50 to 100 percent per annum. For that to occur, if the consensus view of demand elasticities is correct, the relative prices of their exports in world markets would have had to have declined precipitously. But that never occurred. Furthermore, if the price elasticity of demand were as low as is commonly believed, a fairly stable relationship should be observed between LDC export growth and income growth in developed countries, their major export markets. But that is also not observed (Riedel, 1984).

What, then, explains the inconsistency between the observed behavior of LDC exports and what econometric estimates of demand parameters imply about their behavior? Perhaps the answer is that most econometric estimates are misleading because they almost invariably ignore the supply of exports by conveniently assuming it to be infinitely elastic. As shown elsewhere (Riedel, 1988a), if one estimates Hong Kong's export demand function with the usual assumption of infinitely elastic supply, one gets the usual elasticity results. If, however, one estimates the Hong Kong export demand function as part of a simultaneous system of supply and demand equations, one gets very different results: namely, that Hong Kong is a price-taker in world markets. To suggest that Hong Kong is a "small country", albeit the developing world's leading exporter of manufactures, does not seem very remarkable, and it is not except in relation to the consensus view about the demand parameters for LDC manufactured exports.

The threat of protection in developed countries, as a deterrent to LDC export expansion, is also somewhat more apparent than real. The divergence between perception and reality has two sources: one is confusion between the rhetoric of protectionism and the actual implementation of protectionist measures; the second is confusion between the enactment of protectionist measures and their impact.

It is difficult not to be alarmed about a "rising tide of protection" given the prominence of xenophobia in the politics of the Western democracies. And yet, the bark of protectionism is clearly less than its bite, as numerous studies have shown (Gard and Riedel, 1980; Balassa and Balassa, 1984; Hughes and Krueger, 1984; Nogues, Olechowski, and Winters, 1986; Balassa, 1988b). Tariff barriers to LDC exports have steadily fallen, but non-tariff barriers (NTBs) have gone up. However, as of 1985, only 12.9 percent of LDC exports to the US, 21.8 percent of those to the EEC, and 10.5 percent of those to Japan were subject to NTBs (Balassa, 1988a). It is of course difficult to interpret these measures since they are subject to bias in both directions. On the one hand, if NTBs are effective in limiting imports, weighting their incidence by the volume of imports involved understates their restrictiveness. At the same time, if the measures are non-binding, the weighting procedure overstates their restrictiveness.

Measuring the impact of NTBs is as problematic as measuring their incidence. Developing countries have found many ingenious ways of getting around them, especially the most common form of NTB, the voluntary export restraint (VER). By up-grading quality, altering product specifications, trans-shipping through third countries, and directly investing in countries with unused quotas, many of the leading LDC exporters have made VERs a very porous form of protection (Baldwin, 1982; Pearson, 1983).

Because of the intractable problem of measuring either the incidence or the effect of NTBs *ex ante*, most analysts have had to assess their impact on the basis of LDC export performance *ex post*. The following quote from Hughes and Krueger (1984) is representative of the conclusion reached by those who have examined the issue:

> Based on the export performance of the developing countries in manufactured goods during the 1970s, it is difficult to infer that increasing protection was the dominant factor at work... The rate of increase of LDC market shares was sufficiently great that it is difficult to imagine that rates would have been significantly higher in the absence of any protectionist measures.

If in the developed countries the threshold for tolerance of LDC imports has not yet been crossed, would it be crossed if the EP strategy were adopted worldwide? One who believes it would is William Cline (1982), who bases his conclusion on a (statistically insignificant) regression model for predicting the incidence of protection against LDC exports. The weakness of his case in favor of the "fallacy of composition" argument lies not so much in his poor econometric results as in his underlying assumption that all things (including the commodity composition of LDC exports and the level and composition of LDC imports) remain equal as all LDCs emulate the Hong Kong experience. Even though this argument is patently absurd and has been thoroughly demolished in the literature (Ranis, 1985; Riedel, 1987; Balassa, 1988b), it retains currency among those who view the world economy as a zero-sum game and are prepared to see protectionist measures undertaken which make their prophecy self-fulfilling. Therefore, as Bhagwati (1988, p. 42) reminds us, "In assessing the extent to which the protectionist threat must be taken seriously, one may first make the prudential statement that it should never be regarded lightly".

Non-economic determinants of EP success

There is a saying: "success has many fathers, failure has none." Neoclassical economics may claim the paternity of success in East Asia, but so do others and in doing so they deny the importance of "getting prices right" as a lesson for other countries. Some claim the East Asian success is due to culture, others attribute it to the kind of government those countries have rather than the policies they pursued.

Many argue that what distinguishes the East Asian NICs and makes replication of their experience impossible is a culture that favors diligence, loyalty, hard work, and a strong appreciation of education. It is true these attributes appear to be more abundant in the East Asian NICs than elsewhere. Since these countries share a common Confucian heritage, it may be natural to look for the explanation in culture, a factor relegated to the dustbin of development economics for more than three decades, but currently enjoying an appeal broad enough to embrace the likes of futurologist Herman Kahn (1979) and mathematical economist Michio Morishima (1982).

There are however at least two crucial weaknesses in the cultural explanation for Asian diligence and hard work. First, Confucianism is cited as frequently as the reason for economic stagnation in Asia before the 1960s as it is for economic dynamism thereafter (Needham, 1954; Baum, 1982; Han, 1984). Secondly, attributes of diligence and hard work depend as much as anything on the availability of jobs and the reward given for effort, both of which are generally greater in East Asia than elsewhere in the developing world, thanks, some would say, to being more open economies and putting more reliance on the market incentives.

The importance of political organization and the administrative competence of government, on the other hand, cannot be overstated. After sifting through the accumulated historical evidence on 100 years of development in 42 contemporary developing countries, Reynolds (1983, p. 976) concluded that this is "the single most important explanatory variable [of successful economic development]." An examination of the postwar development of the Asian NICs reached the same conclusion (Riedel, 1988b). There is little room for debate about this, but where there is wide disagreement is about what it means. Some (e.g. Pack and Westphal, 1986; Wade, 1988) interpret this as a refutation of neo-classical economic doctrine, on the mistaken premise that the latter is equivalent to *laissez-faire*. Nothing could be farther from the truth, as Keynes (1926, p. 20) made clear: "the phrase *laissez-faire* is not to be found in the works of Adam Smith, of Ricardo or of Malthus. Even the idea is not present in a dogmatic form in any of the authors."[1] As Smith (1776, p. 651) explains:

> the sovereign has only three duties to attend to: three duties of great importance, indeed, but plain and intelligible to common understandings: first, the duty of protecting society from the violence and invasion of other independent societies; secondly, the duty of establishing an exact administration of justice; and thirdly, the duty of erecting and maintaining certain public works and certain public institutions, which it can never be in the interest of any individual, or small number of individuals, to erect and maintain.

To this list, Adam Smith might add, were he writing about contemporary developing countries, the duty of the sovereign to maintain a stable macroeconomic environment.

These four duties the governments of the East Asian NICs have fulfilled reasonably well, and probably better than the governments of most other developing countries. They have also gone beyond these duties, establishing public enterprises to produce private goods and intervening in markets to influence incentives, but whether they have succeeded because of, or inspite of, these activities is by no means clear. It is more apparent, from their experience and from that of other countries where efforts at trade liberalization failed (e.g. Chile and Sri Lanka in the 1970s), that the East Asian countries would not have been nearly as successful had they not adequately fulfilled the minimal functions of government, especially the function of maintaining macroeconomic stability.

Debating whether the key to success in Asia or elsewhere is culture, politics or economics is fruitless. For as E. L. Jones (1981) suggests, growth and development work more like a giant combination lock for which there is no one key. A number of tumblers must fall into place to unlock growth, and one of them perhaps is a minimally rational economic system. The point is sharply put in Peter Timmer's (1973) famous quip: "Getting relative prices right is not the end of development. But getting prices wrong often is."

The timing of liberalization

Few economists would dispute that countries should "get prices right", but some argue that it should not be done while a macroeconomic stabilization program is in progress. As Sachs (1987, p. 293) states: "The success stories of East Asia, so frequently pointed to as illustrations of the benefits of export led growth, do not demonstrate the utility of trade liberalization in the midst of a macroeconomic crisis". As he correctly points out, in Japan, South Korea, and Taiwan, liberalization, such as it was, occurred only after macro-economic stability was achieved. Furthermore, Sachs suggests that "the attempt to stimulate exports at all costs through trade liberalization or aggressive depreciation of the exchange rate can often undermine a stabilization program and thus postpone a resolution of debt crisis" (p. 294). The reason he gives is this: "The current focus on liberalization is distracting attention from the more urgent needs of the debtor countries by overloading the political circuits in those countries and by misdirecting the energies and attention of the international community" (p. 294).

To present trade liberalization as an alternative to fiscal and monetary control, or even a necessary ingredient of a stabilization package, is to set up a straw man. The record is clear that macroeconomic stability is more a requirement for successful liberalization than the reverse. Macro-stability and a very illiberal trade regime are perfectly compatible, as the Indian experience clearly demonstrates. What is not so obvious is that trade liberalization necessarily undermines rather than enhances an otherwise sound stabilization program.

The Turkish experience after 1980 is instructive. At the height of a debt crisis (1978–80) every bit as severe as that experienced by the Latin American debtors, Turkey implemented a stabilization program incorporating all the orthodox prescriptions, including the elimination of quantitative restrictions on imports, a massive real depreciation of the currency and unification of the exchange rate. The results in terms of lowering inflation, restoring growth and expanding exports, which in only five years went from 2 percent to 15 percent of GNP, were astounding. It is premature to declare the Turkish experiment a complete success since inflation has accelerated in recent years and threatens to undo the progress that has been made. However, there is no question that rapid expansion of both exports and imports allowed Turkey to adjust with more growth and less austerity than has been possible in Latin America.[2] Furthermore, there is no evidence that the recent resurgence of inflation is in any way due to trade liberalization; it is earned the old fashion way, by monetizing fiscal deficits (Riedel, 1988c).

Another important lesson the Turkish experience suggests is that, while trade liberalization may not be a necessary part of solving a macroeconomic crisis, a macroeconomic crisis may be, if not necessary, at least highly conducive to the undertaking of trade liberalization. It is hard to imagine that Turkish leaders would have been willing to break with fifty years of *etatism*, which carried the all-important imprimatur of the great Ataturk, had they not found themselves, as they did in 1980, in a near-catastrophic state of economic and political chaos. The need for shock treatment to break down political resistance to trade liberalization is apparently widespread. A series of case studies of the timing and sequencing of trade liberalization carried out under the auspices of the World Bank found that "liberalizations implemented under extreme duress are more likely to succeed than those starting from a 'normal' economic performance" (Michaely, 1988, p. 6). By this criterion, the opportunities for successful liberalization and export promotion should abound.

Consolidating victory

To conclude, the debate between proponents of the IS and EP strategies has been decided, but not on the basis of the relative strength of their theoretical arguments, rather on the basis of what has been found to work in the real world. The debate has therefore left open the question of whether there are alternative strategies that may be superior to those that have been tried, such as that special case of the EP strategy, free trade. Also left open is the question of whether the IS strategy is necessary in the first stage of industrialization, since in practice it was invariably the initial strategy adopted. This issue, however, is not only one of historical interest, but is also of practical significance to those countries which may not have yet completed the "easy phase" of import substitution.

Skirmishes will no doubt continue over the issue of whether external demand is a binding constraint on growth in developing countries. Past experience suggests that believing demand to be a binding constraint, and acting on that belief by adopting inward-looking trade policies, makes it a self-fulfilling prophesy. In order to put this issue to rest, however, much more careful empirical analysis of supply and demand parameters for LDC exports is required.

The protectionist threat to LDC exports will always be an illusive issue. But for developing countries, perhaps the more important question is what they themselves can do to restore faith in the liberal trading system. In the past, developing countries insisted that the rules of the international trading system should not apply to themselves and took advantage of this freedom to construct complex systems of protection with the aim, in part, of breaking the supposed external constraint on their development. However, to the extent that their demand for exemption from the rules has given reason or excuse to the developed countries to break the rules, the constraint has only resurfaced in another form.

Finally, it should be acknowledged that there remains at least one vast area of the globe over which the EP strategy does not hold sway, even in the minds of many professional economists. That is, of course, Africa. The contest between the IS strategy and the EP strategy was fought elsewhere, mainly in the newly industrializing countries, where the contrasting experiences of industrialization under each strategy offered relatively clear, unambiguous lessons. But are those lessons relevant to Africa, where industrialization has barely begun and where the obstacles to progress seem so overwhelming and largely unrelated to the issues at stake in the IS–EP debate?

Even if the lessons are relevant, it does not mean that they will necessarily work the same magic in Africa that they have elsewhere. However, one should not confuse a policy with its outcome. The export promotion strategy is defined by a certain structure of relative incentives, not by any given rate of export growth. The incentive structure associated with the export promotion strategy may be (and probably is) as appropriate in Africa as it is elsewhere, even though it may not (and probably would not) yield results that are at all comparable to those obtained elsewhere. Unfortunately this point is often lost in the vain search for the "key" to progress in Africa and other regions that lag behind, a key that more often than not seems to lie in the realms of culture and politics than in economics. Trade policy will therefore remain a contentious issue, and many battles will be waged before the victory of the EP strategy is consolidated.

Notes

1 Lal (1983), in his brilliant exposé of the "poverty of development economics," makes this point and gives the quote from Keynes.

2 True to Bhagwati's Law, Sachs (1985) dismisses the role of export growth in allowing Turkey to achieve adjustment with growth, attributing it instead to official capital inflows from NATO countries worried about Middle East stability. It is

doubtful, however, that those inflows would have been forthcoming had Turkey not raised its capacity to manage debt by expanding the share of exports in GNP. *Bhagwati's Law*: "economic miracles are a public good; each economist sees in them a vindication of his pet theories" (1987, p. 285).

References

Balassa, Bela. 1971. *The Structure of Protection in Developing Countries*, Baltimore: The Johns Hopkins University Press.

Balassa, Bela. 1978. Exports and economic growth: further evidence. *Journal of Development Economics*, (June) 181–9.

Balassa, Bela. 1988a. U.S. trade policy towards developing countries. Symposium on New Directions in Trade Policy, Johns Hopkins University School of Advanced International Studies, 21 October 1988.

Balassa, Bela. 1988b. The adding up problem. The World Bank PPR Working Paper Series, no. 30.

Balassa, Bela, and Carol Balassa. 1984. Industrial protection in the developed countries. *World Economy*, (June) 179–96.

Baldwin, Robert. 1982. *The Inefficacy of Trade Policy*. Essays in International Finance 150. Princeton University.

Baum, R. 1982. Science and culture in contemporary China: the roots of retarded modernization. *Asian Survey* 1(12), 1166–86.

Bautista, Romeo M. 1988. Agriculture-based development strategy: issues and policy framework, unpublished mimeo. Washington, DC: International Food Policy Research Institute.

Bhagwati, Jagdish. 1978. *Anatomy and Consequences of Exchange Control Regimes*. Cambridge, MA: Ballinger, for the NBER.

Bhagwati, Jagdish. 1988. Export-promoting trade strategy: issues and evidence. *The World Bank Research Observer*, (January) 27–57.

Cline, William. 1982. Can the East Asian model be generalized? *World Development* 10(2), 81–90.

Donges, Jurgen, and James Riedel, 1977. Expansion of manufactured exports in developing countries: an empirical assessment of supply and demand issues. *Weltwirtschaftliches Archiv*. (May) 58–87.

Feder, G. 1983. On exports and economic growth, *Journal of Development Economics* (February/April) 59–74.

Feenstra, Robert C. 1984. Voluntary export restraint in US autos, 1980–81: quality, employment and welfare effects, in Robert E. Baldwin and Anne O. Krueger (eds), *The Structure and Evolution of Recent US Trade Policy*, Chicago: University of Chicago Press, pp. 35–59.

Gard, Linda, and James Riedel. 1980. Safeguard protection of industry in developed countries: assessment of the implications for developing countries. *Weltwirtschaftliches Archiv*. (Heft 3) 471–92.

Goldstein, M., and M. Khan. 1985. Income and price effects in foreign trade. In

R. W. Jones and P. Kenen, eds, *Handbook of International Economics*, vol. 2. Amsterdam: Elsevier.

Han, S. S. 1984. Of economic success and Confucianism. *Far Eastern Economic Review* 126(51), 104–6.

Hughes, H., and A. Krueger. 1984. Effects of protection in developed countries on developing countries. In R. Baldwin and A. Krueger, eds, *The Structure and Evolution of Recent U.S. Trade Policy*. Chicago: University of Chicago Press, for the NBER.

Jones, E. L. 1981. *The European Miracle: Environments, Economies, and Geopolitics in the History of Europe and Asia*, New York: Cambridge University Press.

Kahn, H. 1979. *World Economic Development*, Boulder: Westview Press.

Keynes, J. M. 1926. *The End of Laissez Faire*. London: Hogarth Press.

Khanna, Sri Ram. 1988. India's apparel export industry, *Textile Outlook International*, 18, pp. 8–23.

Krueger, Anne O. 1978. *Foreign Trade Regimes and Economic Development: Liberalization Attempts and Consequences*. Cambridge, MA: Ballinger, for the NBER.

Krueger, A. 1984. Trade policies in developing countries. In R. Jones and P. B. Kenen, eds, *Handbook of International Economics*. New York: North Holland.

Krueger, A., and B. Tuncer. 1982. An empirical test of the infant industry argument. *American Economic Review*, (June) 1142–52.

Krugman, Paul. 1986. New trade theory and the less developed countries. Paper presented at the Carlos Diaz-Alejandro Memorial Conference. World Institute for Development Economics Research. Helsinki.

Lal, Deepak, 1983. *The Poverty of Development Economics*. London: Institute of International Affairs.

Lal, Deepak, 1988. Markets, mandarins and mathematicians. *Cato Journal*, forthcoming.

Lal, D., and S. Rajapatirana. 1987. Trade regimes and economic growth in developing countries. *World Bank Research Observer*, (July) 189–217.

Lewis, W. A. 1980. The slowing down of the engine of growth. *American Economic Review*, (September) 555–64.

Little, I. M. D. 1982. *Economic Development: Theory, Policy and International Relations*. New York: Basic Books.

Little, I. M. D., T. Scitovsky, and M. Scott. 1970. *Industry and Trade in Some Developing Countries*. London: Oxford University Press.

Michaely, M. 1977. Exports and growth: an empirical investigation. *Journal of Development Economics*, (March) 49–53.

Michaely, M. 1988. Trade liberalization policies: lessons of experience, unpublished mimeo. The World Bank.

Michalopoulos, C., and K. Jay. 1973. Growth of exports and income in developing world: a neo-classical view. Washington, DC: Agency for International Development Discussion Paper 28.

Morishima, M. 1982. *Why has Japan Succeeded? Western Technology and the Japanese Ethos*. Cambridge: Cambridge University Press.

Needham, J. 1954. *Science and Civilization in China*. Cambridge: Cambridge University Press.

Nogues, J. J., A. Olechowski, and L. A. Winters. 1986. The extent of non-tariff barriers to industrial countries' imports. *World Bank Economic Review*, (September) 181–98.

Pack, Howard. 1986. The links between development strategies and industrial growth, unpublished mimeo. The World Bank.

Pack, H., and L. E. Westphal. 1986. Industrial strategy and technological change: theory and evidence. *Journal of Development Economics*. 22, 87–128.

Pearson, C. 1983. *Emergency Protection in the Footwear Industry*. Thames Essay No. 36, London: Trade Policy Research Centre.

Ranis, G. 1985. Can the East Asian model of development be generalized: a comment, *World Development* 13 (April), 533–45.

Reynolds, L. G. 1983. The spread of economic growth to the Third World: 1850–1980. *Journal of Economic Literature* 21(3), 941–80.

Riedel, James. 1984. Trade as an engine of growth, revisited. *Economic Journal*, (March) 56–73.

Riedel, James. 1987. *Myths and Realities of External Constraints on Development*. London: Gower, for the Trade Policy Research Centre.

Riedel, James. 1988a. The demand for LDC exports of manufactures: estimates from Hong Kong. *Economic Journal*, (March) 138–48.

Riedel, James. 1988b. Economic development in East Asia: doing what comes naturally? In H. Hughes, ed., *Achieving Industrialization in East Asia*. London: Cambridge University Press.

Riedel, James. 1988c. Macroeconomic crises and long-term economic growth in developing countries: a case study of Turkey, Part II, unpublished mimeo. The Johns Hopkins University, School of Advanced International Studies (May).

Sachs, J. 1985. External debt and macroeconomic performance in Latin America and East Asia. *Brookings Papers on Economic Activity*, 2, 523–64.

Sachs, J. 1987. Trade and exchange rate policies in growth-oriented adjustment programs. In V. Corbo, M. Goldstein, and M. Khan, eds, *Growth-Oriented Adjustment Programs*. Washington DC: International Monetary Fund, 291–325.

Smith, A. 1776. *The Wealth of Nations*.

Srinivasan, T. N. 1986a. Development strategy: is the success of outward orientation at an end? In S. Guhan and M. Shroff, eds, *Essays on Economic Progress and Welfare*. New Delhi: Oxford University Press.

Srinivasan, T. N. 1986. Recent theories of imperfect competition and international trade: any implications for development strategy? unpublished mimeo. The World Bank.

Timmer, C. P. 1973. Choice of technique in rice milling in Java. *Bulletin of Indonesian Studies*. 9(2), 57–76.

Tyler, William. 1981. Growth and export expansion in developing countries: some empirical evidence. *Journal of Development Economics*. 9(1), 121–30.

Wade, R. 1988. The role of government in overcoming market failure: Taiwan, South Korea and Japan. In H. Hughes, ed., *Achieving Industrialization in East Asia*. Cambridge: Cambridge University Press.

Westphal, L. E. 1982. Fostering technological mastery by means of selective infant industry protection. In M. Syrquin and S. Teitel, eds, *Trade, Stability, Technology and Equity in Latin America*. New York: Academic Press.

Part III

The Practice of Trade Policy

8

Transitional Measures in Trade Liberalization

*Wendy E. Takacs**

Introduction

One of the fundamental goals of trade policy since the Second World War has been the establishment and maintenance of a system of world trade based on a multilateral nondiscriminatory trading system in which tariffs would be the primary instruments of trade policy, and trade would be expanded through reciprocal tariff reductions. Other types of trade restrictions, particularly discriminatory quantitative trade restrictions, would be eliminated over time until they were used in only very limited circumstances, such as balance of payments crises or as a necessary complement to domestic agricultural support policies.

Although the conversion of most trade barriers in the industrialized countries to tariffs after the war and subsequent progress toward reducing these tariffs has been laudable, recent years have witnessed serious backsliding with the proliferation of "managed trade" through export restraint arrangements, such as the Japanese voluntary export restraint (VER) on automobile shipments to the United States from 1981 through 1985, and the current steel arrangements. Important segments of trade between industrialized and developing countries have also fallen prey to quantitative trade restrictions. The most notable of these is the Multi-Fiber Arrangement (MFA).

Some of these quantitative restrictions were only temporary detours, such as the Japanese auto VER, or the VERs negotiated by the United States to protect the television and shoe industries through the escape clause mechanism. Others are still with us, however, albeit in modified form. The 1957 VRA with Japan on cotton textile exports became the Short Term Arrangement Regarding International Trade in Cotton Textiles in 1961, which became the Long Term Arrangement in 1962, and the first Multi-Fiber Arrangement in 1974. We are now well into the fourth MFA. The Japanese and European VERs on steel exports to the US that were in effect from 1969 through 1974 went through a brief metamorphosis as the trigger price mechanism before emerging again in 1982, this time in the form of a VRA with European producers, which has grown since then to cover trade with 28 countries.

Many developing countries still use quantitative restrictions as the primary method of restricting trade, controlling the balance of payments, and protecting domestic industries.

Both the longstanding protective measures in developing countries and the *ad hoc*, but more or less continuous, protective measures for declining industries in the industrialized countries distort resource allocation and create vested interests to continue the restrictive measures. For reasons discussed in the next section, the distortions can become particularly acute and the created vested interests particularly strong and vociferous when the trade barriers are quantitative in nature. Dismantling these barriers overnight could lead to severe adjustment problems both for protected import-competing industries and possibly also for supplying industries in exporting countries that currently benefit from the discriminatory nature of many of the restrictions.

Nonetheless, removing or phasing out quantitative restrictions, returning to trade based on tariffs alone, and then in turn reducing these tariffs over time, is still a worthwhile ultimate goal. The issue then becomes one of how to attain that goal. This chapter notes problems that can arise during the process of dismantling quantitative restrictions and suggests alternative transitional measures that could be used to transform a system of quantitative restrictions into a tariffs-only regime. The second section explains some of the arguments for switching from quantitative restrictions to tariffs and points out why transitional measures may be useful. The next four sections discuss, in turn, four possible mechanisms for dismantling quantitative restrictions and liberalizing trade: (1) gradually increasing the quota ceilings and then eliminating the quotas when they become nonbinding; (2) converting quotas immediately to tariffs and then reducing the tariff rates; (3) auctioning quota licenses as an interim measure; and (4) converting quotas to tariff-quotas and then liberalizing the tariff-quotas.

The nature of the problem

Virtually all international economists would agree that tariffs are preferable to quantitative restrictions, for a variety of reasons. First, tariffs distort resource allocation by directly increasing the prices of imported goods, but the distortionary effect is limited in the sense that the deviation of the domestic price from the world price is limited to the tariff rate. Quotas, on the other hand, sever any links between the domestic and foreign markets. Once the quota ceiling is reached, no more imports can enter, no matter how large the discrepancy between world market prices and domestic production costs. The distortions to resource allocation can become increasingly severe as competitive conditions change.

Severing the link between world market and domestic prices also allows domestic industries to exercise any market power they may have. If the domestic industry is made up of a small number of firms, or in the extreme just one firm,[1] the fact that imports cannot exceed the quota ceiling implies that the domestic producer or producers (collectively) need not be concerned about losing any additional sales to foreign competitors if they increase their prices. This allows the domestic industry to exploit the monopoly or oligopoly power that was given by the quota. With a tariff, on the other hand, the quantity imported can always increase as long as the importer pays the import duty, so domestic market power is not increased. Tariffs are thus preferable to quotas because they do not enhance the monopoly power of concentrated domestic industries (Corden, 1974, p. 208).

In addition to limiting the price increasing effect of the restriction, it is argued that tariffs are more "transparent" than quotas. That is, the price increasing effect is more obvious and more easily quantifiable. A tariff is a tax; the revenue goes to the government. It is quite clear, at least to the importer who pays the tax, that his or her costs are increased. Quotas drive up domestic prices indirectly, by limiting supply. The effect is not as obvious nor as easily measured in the absence of data on the prices at which restricted imported goods sell to final users (which can then be compared with import prices), or the prices at which exporting countries sell to nonrestrained markets (which can then be compared with the prices at which they sell to the restrained market). Such data are seldom readily available. Anti-protectionist forces can more easily battle a visible enemy.

A third reason why tariffs are generally favored over quotas has to do with the discriminatory nature of quotas. If import quotas cover all suppliers, they are often divided up among supplying countries. Thus they not only arbitrarily divide the market between domestic and foreign suppliers, but also among potential exporting countries, usually on historic or political grounds, without any reference to current competitive or relative cost considerations. Voluntary export restraints can be expected to have even more perverse effects on resource allocation, because they generally are negotiated only with the countries that are perceived to be "troublemakers," not because they have a large share of the market, but because they have a growing share of the market. Thus there is a systematic bias against imports from the most efficient suppliers. Tariffs, on the other hand, are normally applied on a most-favored-nation (MFN) basis, so that the same tariff is levied on imports from all sources. The tariff encourages using the lowest-cost suppliers.

A fourth difference between *ad valorem* tariffs and quotas that restrict imports to a particular quantity is that the quota will encourage a shift in the composition of imports toward higher-valued items.[2] This may impose a disproportionate burden on lower-income consumers, as the varieties that they would choose disappear from the market. It may also undermine the protective intent of the quota, as import-competing firms at the "upper end" of the market face relatively greater import competition, while producers of lower priced varieties receive proportionately greater protection.

A fifth reason to favor tariffs over quotas is the fiscal effect of a tariff. Both quotas and tariffs increase the prices of the restricted imports and domestic import-competing substitutes. The consumers or users of the product are hurt. With tariffs, at least part of the revenue associated with higher prices goes to the government in the form of tariff revenue. This increased government revenue may be of particular importance to developing countries, many of which rely on tariff revenue as a large proportion of total government revenue. It would also be of interest to a post-Gramm-Rudman United States.

This revenue can either be used to lower taxes or provide more public services, so the transfers that take place when tariffs are imposed in most cases will be general: from a large number of consumers to a large number of taxpayers or recipients of public services. It is unlikely that the two groups will exactly correspond, but consumers may be at least in part compensated for the loss due to the price increases.

With quotas, the transfer is more concentrated. Prices increase to all consumers of the restricted goods, but the gainers will be those individuals or firms able to import the item either because they managed to bring it in before the ceiling was reached and customs authorities allowed no more imports, or because they received licenses to import, which also are often distributed according to historic import levels or according to bureaucratic discretion. Thus, in general, equity considerations make tariffs preferable to quotas.

Equity considerations, however, do not always favor tariffs over quotas, or a conversion of existing quantitative restrictions to tariffs. When the quantitative restrictions are administered in the exporting country, there is reason to believe that the windfall gains accrue to the exporters. When developing countries are the exporters, and industrialized countries the importers, the switch from quotas to tariffs may transfer income from poorer to richer nations. Conversion of US sugar quotas or the MFA, for example, to a tariff regime could result in what could be considered significant reverse foreign aid flows.[3]

The windfall gains to the recipients of quota licenses can also waste resources because there is an incentive for individuals to use up real resources trying to compete for the rents. While it has been argued that the revenue from tariffs engenders the same type of behavior, the more direct and certain gains with quotas probably do encourage more activity of this type.

One last reason for liberal traders to favor tariffs over quotas is that in successive rounds of trade negotiations it has been possible to negotiate formulas for across-the-board tariff reduction. Experience has shown that it is possible to liberalize trade controlled by tariffs on a reciprocal basis. This again was one of the fundamental cornerstones of the GATT system. While it is conceivable that quantitative restrictions might be liberalized on a reciprocal basis, they appear less conducive to such treatment. Thus proponents of trade liberalization see a conversion of quantitative restrictions to tariffs as a first step toward eventual downward negotiation of the tariff rates.

For all of the reasons cited above, removing quantitative restrictions and returning to trade based on tariffs alone is a worthwhile goal, on both efficiency and equity grounds. Simply abolishing quantitative restrictions overnight would be one policy option. Such a move would not be unprecedented. Greece, for example, eliminated its quantitative restrictions on most products virtually overnight, with beneficial overall effects (Papageorgiou, 1988).

It is unlikely, however, that a policy of immediately removing quantitative restrictions will be attractive to policymakers. Longstanding systems of quantitative restrictions have so distorted resource allocation that the adjustment costs, in terms of short-run unemployment and relocation costs, are likely to render the option politically unacceptable. A sudden increase in imports, or even a sudden change in the product composition, could cause severe "disruption" of the domestic industry because of a sudden decrease in sales that would displace labor, cause long periods of involuntary unemployment and losses to owners of capital specific to the import-competing industry. Quantitative restrictions also create other vested interests. Recipients of quota licenses, and even exporting countries favored by the quota allocation procedures, would also oppose their removal. A country on a fixed exchange rate also would have to be concerned about the potential balance of payments problems that would be caused by a large, sudden increase in imports.

Ideally, it would be advantageous if the removal of quantitative trade restrictions could be conducted in a way that would avoid abrupt, very large shifts in the volume, composition, or geographical pattern of trade. This would help make the adjustment to freer trade under a tariffs-only regime more gradual, thus lowering adjustment costs. It would also help prevent the balance of payments problems that might arise if imports accelerated rapidly before the economy had time to accomplish the structural adjustments that would expand exports. It might also help obtain political support for trade liberalization, or at least reduce the intensity of the political pressure against it.[4] In any event, it is clear that the revealed preference of policy makers is for gradual removal of quantitative measures.[5]

However, the transitional measures must at the same time ensure that in the end trade actually will be liberalized and controlled by binding tariffs rather than by quantitative measures. If the transitional measures are too timid or too drawn out, they might have the effect of postponing forever the actual liberalization.

Well-designed transitional measures may enhance the credibility of a liberalization program. Expectations of a reversal of the program because of problems and disruptions may make it more difficult for a liberalization program to succeed.[6]

It would also be useful if the transitional measures themselves provided some information along the way about the degree of restrictiveness of the remaining quantitative restrictions or the tariff that would duplicate the trade effects of the quotas.

The remainder of this chapter discusses four possible methods of removing or phasing out quantitative restrictions. The following sections examine in turn:

1 expanded quotas;
2 immediate conversion of quotas to tariffs;
3 auction quotas; and
4 tariff-quotas.

It should be noted that these approaches are not necessarily mutually exclusive. Australia's trade liberalization, for example, has used tariff-quotas in which the quota component has been expanded, the licenses to import within quota at a lower tariff rate have been auctioned, and the penalty (higher) tariff rate has been reduced over time. The measures are discussed here separately to explain how each could be used alone and to point out some advantages and disadvantages of each.

Liberalizing quotas

Perhaps the most straightforward method of phasing out quantitative restrictions would be to gradually increase the quota ceilings.[7] If the volume of imports allowed in under the quota increases sufficiently, it eventually will reach the point at which the quantity that would be imported in the absence of the quota is less than the quota ceiling, so the quota becomes "nonbinding", and the binding restriction would be any remaining tariffs on the product.

Such a liberalization could be administered by declaring a given growth rate in the quota limits per year. The growth rate in the ceilings could be modest at first, for example, 5 or 10 percent. To ensure that the quotas would eventually become nonbinding, the growth rate could escalate in ensuing years to rates that would undoubtedly exceed the growth rate of domestic demand, such as 100, 500, and 1000 percent.

This method of gradually increasing the quota ceilings is straightforward and simple, and will eventually return trade to a tariffs-only system provided that the rate of growth of the quota limits outpaces growth in domestic demand, and nothing increases cost conditions in the importing countries, so that the quota eventually becomes nonbinding. Moreover, it has the advantage of liberalizing during the transition period.

Gradually increasing the quota ceilings, everything else held constant, will also gradually decrease the difference between domestic and import price. This will gradually reduce the incentive for upgrading, so the composition of imports should also shift slowly, avoiding any sudden pressure on domestic firms producing lower-valued items.

One practical problem is the criterion for deciding when the quota is considered nonbinding, so that it can be eliminated. One possible method would be to watch the quantity of imports and compare it with the quota ceiling. When the quantity actually imported falls below the quota ceiling, one would then be tempted to conclude that the point had been reached where the quota could be eliminated without causing any large, sudden change in the volume of trade.

It is not clear, however, that a quota has no effect on trade if imports do not reach the quota ceiling. The existence of a quota ceiling, even if imports currently do not reach the ceiling, can act as "insurance" for the domestic industry. It reduces the uncertainty surrounding the prospect for future sales, and thus may encourage investment in the domestic industry, while discouraging marketing attempts by foreign firms, or investment abroad to supply this particular export market. Removing the quota would eliminate the certain market for the domestic industry while at the same time offering an expanded market to firms abroad. The volume of imports could increase as a result.

A quota could also be nonbinding because the method of administering the quota arrangements had bestowed monopoly power on the importer or exporter, who found it profitable to "shortship," that is, restrict imports to below the quota ceiling to drive up price and increase profits. Eliminating the quota system would eliminate the monopoly power, and, again, imports would increase if the quota were abolished even though it appeared to be nonbinding.

Another issue is how to handle the expansion of quota ceilings when the overall quota is subdivided among individual supplying countries. If the quota system has been in existence for some time, newly emerging suppliers, who may in fact be the most competitive suppliers in the long run, probably have very small, or perhaps no, quota. A given rate of increase in the existing quota ceilings may prolong the adjustment for a very long time. One way to avoid this problem would be to allocate all of the increases in quota ceilings to a global pool, where imports could be from any source. This method seems fitting for quotas administered by the importing country, but is more difficult to implement to liberalize a system of negotiated export quotas. Suppliers with smaller quotas would have to be allowed larger percentage increases.

Immediate conversion to tariffs

Given the superiority of tariffs over quotas, another possibility would be to shift immediately to protection by tariff rather than protection by quota. An immediate conversion to tariffs has been suggested as a method of liberalizing the MFA.[8] The concern with an immediate conversion to tariffs centers around the uncertainty as to exactly what tariff will have the same protective effect as the existing quantitative restriction. If the tariff rates were set too low, imports would increase, possibly forcing more radical adjustment on domestic industries than would be optimal.

A rapid increase in imports also could lead to balance of payments problems. This would be a greater concern to developing countries dismantling their own quota systems than to developed countries liberalizing *ad hoc* protective measures. Balance of payments crises after trade liberalization appear to be a major cause of abandonment or reversal of trade liberalization programs in developing countries.[9]

On the other hand, if the tariff rate is set too high, then the conversion to tariffs could, at least in the short run, result in a greater restriction of trade than the quota. It could also leave trade more restricted in the long run as well, if it proves difficult to reduce tariffs after the conversion.[10]

Given the lack of transparency of quota restrictions, it is not immediately obvious what tariff rate to set to duplicate the effect of the quota. If the restricted product is fairly standardized, if the restriction is in the form of a global import quota, and if all of the firms involved in production and trading are fairly small, so that production, importing and exporting can be treated as competitive industries, then at least in principle there should be a tariff rate that will duplicate the effect of the quota, except for the distribution of the tariff equivalent revenue. A tariff at a rate equal to the percentage difference between the selling price in the domestic market and the import price would approximate the impact of the import quota. Monopoly power in the domestic industry, a monopoly importer, or a single exporter, however, would frustrate this method (see Bhagwati, 1965). In these cases, imposing a tariff equal to the difference between domestic and import price would not duplicate the effect of the quota.

Also, if the quantitative restriction were a "voluntary export restraint" rather than an import quota, the import price would already reflect the price-increasing effect of the restriction, so it would be necessary to use a more roundabout method of estimating the equivalent tariff. Possible methods include ascertaining the difference between the import price and production costs abroad, comparing the exporter's price for exports to the restricted market with the price of exports to a nonrestricted market, and finding the price at which export permits for shipments to the restricted market exchange in the exporting country.

Further complications arise if the restricted product is differentiated or if the quota is subdivided among exporting countries. The expected upgrading under the quantitative restriction would be reversed if an *ad valorem* tariff were imposed instead, which would suddenly change the composition of imports toward lower-valued rather than higher-valued items. This would suddenly reduce the sales of firms specializing in lower-valued items within the domestic industry. Switching to a specific rather than an *ad valorem* tariff would alleviate this problem.

Many import quotas are divided into subquotas for particular exporting countries (US sugar and cheese quotas, for example). It would be impossible to duplicate the effect of these discriminatory quotas without resorting to discriminatory tariffs, which would violate the GATT more flagrantly (although not more fundamentally) than the current set of restrictions. An immediate conversion to MFN tariffs would be opposed by exporting countries that have large quotas on political or historical grounds, but are not as competitive as lower-cost suppliers. In the case of discriminatory export restraints, suppliers not currently covered by the restrictions would have cause for complaint.

For the reasons cited above it may be difficult to accurately set tariffs that would duplicate the volume, value, commodity composition, and geographical pattern of existing quantitative restrictions. If so, it would be difficult to immediately switch *directly* from quotas to tariffs without risking possibly unacceptable costs to the domestic industry and/or favored foreign suppliers, balance of payments problems, or a further restriction, rather than a liberalization, of trade. The next two sections discuss two suggested interim measures: auction quotas and tariff-quotas.

Auction quotas

When quantitative restrictions are administered by issuing licenses or permits to import or export, these are normally distributed to firms free of charge.[11] But the licenses could be sold by the government to the highest bidder, and the bids could provide useful information about the tariff equivalents of the quotas.

Lawrence and Litan (1986, pp. 99–101) suggest a plan to use auction quotas as a transitional measure to convert the set of quantitative restrictions in the MFA to tariffs. In a first stage, the importing countries would convert existing individual country export quotas into one overall import quota for each product category. Importing country governments would then auction off to the highest bidder the permits or licenses to import within these global quotas. In a second stage, these bids would serve as a guide to set tariff rates to replace the quotas with tariffs.[12]

This proposal raises the issue of whether the bids in an auction can be expected to accurately reflect the tariff equivalent of the quota. If they do, then using auction quotas as a transitional measure could avoid mistakes in setting the tariff rates that could either lead to greater restrictiveness or cause adjustment or balance of payments difficulties. If not, then using the bids to set tariff rates could leave sufficient adjustment, or balance of payments problems, to scuttle the liberalization, or end up further restricting rather than liberalizing.

In a long-run competitive equilibrium in which bidders have perfect foresight, the bids that emerge from quota license auctions should give a good approximation of the tariff equivalent of the quotas. The firms or individuals bidding in an auction for the licenses would be willing to bid up to the profit they expect to earn from importing the restricted goods. This would equal the difference between the price at which they could sell in the domestic market and the cost of the imported goods, including transportation costs. Under competitive conditions, a tariff equal to this difference between the domestic price and foreign cost would have the same aggregate effect as the quota.

However, in the short run, or in cases where markets are not competitive, there are reasons to believe that bids might either underestimate or overestimate the size of the quota rents, and thus the tariff equivalent of the quota.[13]

To explain why bids might underestimate the tariff equivalent of the quota, take the case of a monopoly exporter or producer abroad. The quota (either an import quota or a VRA) limits supply to the domestic market and drives up the selling price of the restrained item. Traders would be willing to bid up to the difference between the cost of the goods to them and the domestic selling price. An astute monopoly supplier could increase the price of the product to the traders without decreasing the amount sold, and thus capture the quota rents. The bids would be correspondingly lower, and would not accurately reflect the tariff that would achieve the same import levels. The same phenomenon could occur if the exporting country were to react to the auction by taxing exports. Also, if there were a monopoly importer, or few enough importers to allow collusion, they could expect to prevail in an auction by offering only a token bid.

Bids might also overestimate the size of the equivalent tariff. In the short run, importing firms may have fixed costs associated with distribution facilities or capital equipment to further process imported raw materials or intermediate goods. If these firms do not obtain licenses, and cannot import at all, they would incur losses equal to their fixed costs. In the short run, firms with fixed costs would be willing to bid up to the expected quota rent *plus* the losses they would incur if they could not import at all. Their bids would overestimate the long-run tariff equivalent of the quota.

Strategic bidding might also result in bids greater than the tariff equivalent. Suppose that anyone can bid in the auctions and that the government has announced that it will set a tariff equal to the bids received in the auction. Domestic import-competing firms have an incentive to enter the auctions with high bids in an attempt to obtain continued protection at a high rate. They could expect to resell the licenses or import themselves to make up for part of the cost of the bid, and the rest of the extra cost could be made up for from the profits from the continued protection.

Auction quotas may thus provide useful information and revenue to the government, but they are not likely to provide either revenue or accurate information as to the size of the equivalent tariff if either production or exporting abroad is highly concentrated, and will provide revenue but not accurate information if the importing industry is characterized by high fixed costs or a proclivity to try to influence government policy. Thus auctioning quotas as a transitional measure may not be as appropriate for oil, steel, or automobiles as for textiles or for agricultural products.

Australia and New Zealand have both auctioned import quotas as part of their transitional measures in liberalizing their quota regimes, and India has recently begun auctioning export permits for shipments to markets controlled under the MFA. The results of these auctions provide evidence on another possible problem with using auctions to provide information on the tariff equivalents of quota regimes. The bids received in the auctions can vary greatly over a relatively short period of time.

In Australia, for example, the bids were fairly steady over time for some items, such as textiles, but fluctuated greatly from year to year on others. For footwear, the average bids for 1985 were 100 percent; for 1986, only

1.4 percent; then back up to 31 percent for 1987 (Bergsten et al., 1987, p. 95). In the newly instituted Indian textile export quota auctions, the bids varied from 5 to 74 rupees for the same items.[14] If the bids vary so greatly, it is not clear which to choose as the tariff rate.

Tariff-quotas

Another method for liberalizing quotas and converting them to tariffs would be to use tariff-quotas as a transitional device. Australia has used tariff-quotas to achieve a liberalization of its quantitative restrictions, and at least two variants of the idea of using tariff quotas as an interim measure to liberalize textile trade have been suggested (see Cline, 1987, pp. 257–62; Sampson and Takacs, 1988).

Tariff-quotas operate as a two-tier tariff system. Imports up to a given quantity enter at a low tariff rate; imports above that quantity enter at a higher rate. A hypothetical tariff-quota would let 100,000 units enter at a 10 percent rate; imports over 100,000 would enter at a higher rate, say 50 percent.

Tariff-quotas could be used to gradually liberalize existing quota systems by setting the number of units that enter at the low rate equal to the existing quota ceiling. The rate charged on these "within quota" imports would be the existing tariff rate. For imports above the quota ceiling a higher or "penalty" rate would apply. If this penalty rate were set high enough initially to be prohibitive (that is, to allow no over-quota imports), converting a quota system to a tariff-quota would have no immediate impact on trade. The penalty tariff could then be lowered gradually. As the rate gradually fell, it would at some point become low enough to allow some over-quota imports, and these imports would grow as the penalty rate continued to fall. Once the penalty rate fell to the level of the existing MFN tariff, then the quota would have no effect, and could be eliminated. Tariff-quotas can be used as a transitional measure between an existing quota system and a tariff regime with relatively low risk of unintended disruption, but with fairly high assurance that trade will eventually be liberalized. If the rate for over-quota imports is set high enough at first to allow no, or a very small amount of imports,[15] then the uncertainty about the immediate effect of the liberalization on import volumes will be lessened. The penalty rate could even be set "astronomically high" at first, say, at 1000 percent, and follow a schedule in which it would decline quickly at first until a significant amount of imports would enter, at which point it would decline more slowly.

The tariff-quota concept, with a few modifications, could also be used to liberalize a complicated set of voluntary export restraint arrangements, such as the MFA. As mentioned above, two problems with converting VRA arrangements to tariffs are the transfer of revenue from the exporting to the importing country and the fact that the discriminatory nature of the VRAs would require different tariff rates on imports from different countries to duplicate the effects of the quotas. Tariff-quotas could be designed to gradually transfer revenue and shift market shares among supplying countries during the process of liberalization.

This gradual adjustment could be achieved by replacing the set of export quotas with tariff-quotas administered by the importing countries. The tariff-quota arrangement would apply *only* to imports from those countries currently restrained. Imports from unrestrained sources could continue to enter at MFN rates. The quota limit of the tariff-quota for a particular category (the amount that can be imported at the low rate of duty) could be set at an amount equal to the sum of all imports in that category from all restrained sources. The importing country could then issue licenses or permits to import within the quota limit. These licenses would be "global" in the sense that they could be used to import from any source. To eliminate any immediate loss of market share or revenue by any of the exporting countries, at the beginning of the transition process these licenses could be transferred to the government authorities in the exporting countries in proportion to their previous market shares.[16]

The market shares of the exporting countries could then be allowed to change according to their comparative advantages by gradually decreasing the number of licenses allocated to particular exporting countries. As an illustration, the licenses transferred could start at 100 percent, then decrease by 10 percent per year over ten years, so that each country would receive 90 percent of its original allocation in the second year, 80 percent in the third year, and so on.

The global licenses that were not transferred to particular exporting countries could be used to import from any source. The importing country could choose the method it considered best to distribute the licenses to importers. A quota auction, as discussed above, would be a reasonable method of distributing the licenses. These global licenses would presumably be used to import from the least-cost suppliers of each category of product, so the more competitive exporting countries would find their exports increasing even though their official allocations were dwindling over time, while the less efficient suppliers would find their exports shrinking.

Meanwhile, the penalty-rate part of the tariff-quota would fall toward the MFN rate, and each importing country would find its imports growing as the rate fell. The more competitive exporting countries would find their exports increasing from this expansion of trade as well as from their greater share of the previous trade allowed under the quota system. Eventually trade would be returned to a tariffs-only regime once the penalty rate fell to the MFN rate. Further liberalization could then proceed through downward negotiation of the MFN rates.

One advantage of the tariff-quota option for dismantling VER arrangements, which by their nature require negotiations between importing and exporting countries, is that the liberalization schedule need only be negotiated once to ensure eventual liberalization. In contrast, negotiating a particular rate of increase in the quota ceilings themselves may require renegotiation if demand increases more quickly than the preagreed increase in quantities, especially if the most competitive countries have started out from a very low base.

Summary

Reduced reliance on quantitative trade restrictions is a worthwhile long-run goal, but eliminating quotas overnight may lead to adjustment and balance of payments problems. This paper examines four methods of gradually removing quantitative restrictions or converting them to tariffs.

Simply expanding the quota ceilings until they become nonbinding will eventually liberalize trade if the rate of expansion is sufficiently high. Another benefit is that trade expands immediately; there is no delay, as there may be if quotas are first changed to equivalent tariffs, or tariff-quotas where penalty rates are too high to expand imports significantly. However, there is a risk that abolishing quotas that are apparently nonbinding will cause sudden increases in imports. Import "surges" may cause unnecessarily large immediate shifts in income distribution or unemployment costs. At worst, they may scuttle a liberalization program.

An immediate switch from quotas to equivalent tariffs involves a number of risks. Uncertainty as to the exact tariff equivalent of a given quota implies that the conversion may either increase imports too rapidly or restrict trade even more than the original quota. It may be difficult to reduce tariffs after the conversion. Quantity-limiting quotas on differentiated products would have to be changed to specific rather than *ad valorem* tariffs to avoid sudden shifts in the composition of imports. With discriminatory quotas, avoiding sudden shifts in the geographic pattern of trade would require discriminatory tariffs.

Auctioning quotas as a transitional measure can provide information as to the tariff equivalents of existing quota systems, but bids may overestimate or underestimate the tariff equivalent. Auction quotas alone will not liberalize trade unless converted to tariffs which are subsequently lowered.

Tariff-quotas as transitional devices can be designed to guarantee eventual liberalization (provided the penalty tariff rate declines over time) without risking immediate large shifts in trade volume, composition, or geographic pattern. They also eliminate the risk that the transitional measures will unintentionally increase the restrictiveness of the regime. There may, however, be a delay before liberalization begins if the penalty rate is set too high initially or declines too slowly.

Notes

* The author's research on this topic has been supported by the Trade Policy Division of the World Bank.

1 Monopoly producers are not as unlikely as might be thought. In many developing countries where industrialization is not yet widespread, it is not unusual to find a single producer of a manufactured good, or, given economies of scale in processing, a single refiner or processor of agricultural products. Even in industrialized countries, single producers have obtained protection, although not necessarily by quota. Witness the escape clause protection given to the motorcycle industry in the United States (Harley Davidson) and porcelain-on-steel cookware (General Housewares). In the United States the automobile industry and the steel industry, both textbook examples of highly concentrated industries, have been protected by quantitative restrictions.

2 For evidence that upgrading has occurred in textiles, footwear, steel, and automobiles, see, respectively, Keesing and Wolf (1980, pp. 32–3), Pearson (1983, pp. 36–46) and Aw and Roberts (1986); Mintz (1973); and Feenstra (1984). For explanations of why upgrading occurs, see Falvey (1979), Rodriguez (1979) and, Santoni and Van Cott (1980).

3 U.S. sugar quotas are administered by the Secretary of Agriculture. Certificates of eligibility are issued to officials in the exporting industry who in turn issue them to the shipper. To administer MFA quotas, exporting countries normally issue licenses to producers or exporters. In both cases the administrative control over allocation resides with the exporting country.

4 The opposing argument would be that long, drawn-out procedures for converting quotas to tariffs provide ample time for political pressures to be brought to bear against liberalization. See Krueger (1986).

5 See Halevi (1988, pp. 37–8 and 44). In a survey of 40 structural adjustment loans that included trade liberalization measures, Halevi concludes that strong and immediate measures for quota liberalization or the replacement of quantitative restrictions with tariffs were rarely called for. Instead, policymakers opted for slow removal of quantitative restrictions.

6 Edwards (1984) argues that the speed and order of the liberalization should be set in such a way that expectations of a reversal of the program will be low.

7 Martin Wolf (1985, p. 243) suggests gradually increasing quota ceilings as a second stage of MFA liberalization. The first stage, to last five years, would

increase quotas for small suppliers. The second stage would consist of steadily rising minimum rates of growth for all restraint levels: starting with a 6 percent increase in the fifth year and then 10, 15, 25, 50, and 100 percent in ensuing years. The restraint levels would be abolished thereafter.

8 See Keesing and Wolf (1980, p. 201). They characterize this move as a "more orthodox recommendation" than simply liberalizing the quotas. In a later paper, however, Wolf (1985) discusses the practical problems of an immediate conversion to MFN tariffs.

9 For example, Halevi (1988, pp. 52, 54) reports that Zambia dramatically reversed course after virtually all the trade reforms had been implemented because of a balance of payments problem. Krueger (1978, p. 94) attributes the demise of Ghana's 1966–7 reforms to balance of payments pressures. In both cases the balance of payments pressures were due more to world commodity price movements, inappropriate exchange rate policies and macroeconomic management than to trade liberalization itself. Nonetheless, a rapid increase in imports after quota removal or replacement with too low a tariff rate could cause loss of international reserves and a crisis situation, particularly for countries that do not have changes in the exchange rate as a policy option.

10 Balassa (1986) favors an expansion of quotas over a conversion to tariffs on these grounds.

11 The U.S. cheese quotas are administered by allocating import licenses to firms that had previously imported cheese; licenses to import under the U.S. oil import quotas were distributed to domestic oil refineries (whether they used imported oil or not) in proportion to their output levels. In these cases, the licenses were allocated free of charge. For allocation criteria in export restraints, see Hamilton (1986).

12 The authors do not address directly the rather delicate issue of whether these tariffs would be levied only on imports from currently controlled countries under the MFA or on all imports from all sources, including countries not currently subject to restraints. If they are to be levied on all imports from all sources, this would violate the tariff bindings in the GATT, and presumably would be subject to retaliation by countries whose exports are not restricted in the current MFA. If the tariffs were to apply only to imports from currently controlled sources, this would create a system of discriminatory tariffs, which also would violate the principles of GATT.

13 See Bergsten et al. (1987, pp. 45–8 and appendix A) or Takacs (1987, pp. 13–17), for a more detailed explanation of why in competitive markets the bids should reflect the tariff equivalent of the quota, and why they might not in other market structures.

14 These results are reported in Khanna (1988). It is not clear from the context whether these were the market clearing premia from successive auctions or the individual bids in a single auction. If the former, then the problem of fluctuating bids arises, if the latter, then it might simply reflect the different value of the licenses to different firms, which is to be expected.

15 Exactly how high a penalty rate would be necessary to allow no imports is of course open to question and will require an informed guess. But the point is that

guessing too high does relatively little damage. It would not restrict trade further than it was already restricted; it would simply postpone the liberalization process unnecessarily.

16 Transferring the licenses to the exporting countries also allows them to continue whatever license allocation systems they have in effect. Many countries allocate licenses according to criteria such as export prices, new export products, volume of exports to nonrestrained markets, or previous period's export volumes. See Hamilton (1986) and Khanna (1988) for discussions of quota allocation methods. Another issue is whether the quotas transferred to the exporting countries should be transferable among exporting countries. If they are, the total volume of trade may change as an underutilized quota in one region is transferred to a country where the quota is binding, but the value of the quota licenses to the original recipient country would be greater if it were transferrable in this way.

References

Aw, B. Y., and M. J. Roberts. 1986. Measuring quality change in quota-constrained import markets, *Journal of International Economics*, 21, 45–60.

Balassa, Bela. 1986. The timing and sequencing of a trade liberalization policy: comment. In Armeane M. Choksi and Demetris Papageorgiou, eds, *Economic Liberalization in Developing Countries*. New York: Basil Blackwell.

Bergsten, C. Fred, Kimberly Ann Elliott, Jeffrey J. Schott, and Wendy E. Takacs. 1987. *Auction Quotas and United States Trade Policy*. Washington, DC: Institute for International Economics.

Bhagwati, Jagdish N. 1965. The nonequivalence of tariffs and quotas. In R. E. Baldwin et al., eds, *Trade, Growth, and the Balance of Payments*. Amsterdam: North Holland.

Cline, William R. 1987. *The Future of World Trade in Textiles and Apparel*, Washington, DC: Institute for International Economics.

Corden, W. M. 1974. *Trade Policy and Economic Welfare*, Oxford: Clarendon.

Edwards, Sebastian. 1984. *The Order of Liberalization of the External Sector in Developing Countries*, Princeton Essays in International Finance no. 156 (December).

Falvey, R. 1979. The composition of trade within import-restricted categories, *Journal of Political Economy*, 87(5), 1105–14.

Feenstra, Robert C. 1984. Voluntary Export Restraint in US Autos, 1980–1: Quality, Employment and Welfare Effects. In Robert E. Baldwin and Anne O. Krueger, eds., *The Structure and Evolution of Recent US Trade Policy*. Chicago: University of Chicago Press.

Halevi, Nadav. 1988. Trade liberalization in adjustment lending, unpublished.

Hamilton, Carl. 1986. Asean systems for allocation of export licenses under VERs. In Christopher Findlay and Ross Garnaut, eds, *The Political Economy of Manufacturing Protection: Experiences of Asean and Australia*. Allen and Unwin.

Hufbauer, Gary C., and Jeffrey J. Schott. 1985. *Trading for Growth: The Next Round of Trade Negotiations*, Washington, DC: Institute for International Economics.

Keesing, Donald B., and Martin Wolf. 1980. *Textile Quotas against Developing*

Countries, London: Trade Policy Research Centre.

Khanna, Sri Ram. 1988. India's Apparel Export Industry, *Textile Outlook International*, 18, 8–23.

Krueger, Anne O. 1978. *Liberalization Attempts and Consequences*, Vol. 10 of *Foreign Trade Regimes and Economic Development*, New York: National Bureau of Economic Research.

Krueger, Anne O. 1986. Problems of liberalization. In Armeane M. Choksi and Demetris Papageorgiou, *Economic Liberalization in Developing Countries*, New York: Basil Blackwell.

Lawrence, Robert Z., and Robert E. Litan. 1986. *Saving Free Trade: A Pragmatic Approach*, Washington: The Brookings Institution.

Mintz, Ilse. 1973. *U.S. Import Quotas: Costs and Consequences*, Washington: American Enterprise Institute.

Papageorgiou, Demetris. 1988. Greece: the first attempt at liberalization: the reform of 1953, presented at the Conference for a New Policy Towards Foreign Trade in Brazil, Sao Paulo (April).

Pearson, Charles S. 1983. *Emergency Protection in the Footwear Industry*, Thames Essay 36. London: Trade Policy Research Centre.

Rodriguez, C. 1979. The quality of imports and the differential welfare effects of tariffs, quotas, and quality controls as protective devices, *Canadian Journal of Economics*, 12(3), 439–49.

Sampson, Gary, and Wendy E. Takacs. 1988. Returning textile trade to the normal workings of GATT: a practical proposal for reform, Seminar Paper 404, Institute for International Economic Studies, Stockholm (January).

Santoni, G. J., and T. N. Van Cott. 1980. Import quotas: the quality adjustment problem, *Southern Economic Journal*, 46(4), 1206–11.

Takacs, Wendy E. 1987. Auctioning import quota licenses: an economic analysis, Seminar Paper 390, Institute for International Economic Studies, Stockholm (September).

Wolf, Martin. 1985. How to unravel the multi-fibre arrangement, *World Economy*, 8, 235–47.

World Bank. 1988. Trade liberalization: the lessons of experience, Report No. IDP14 (April).

Index

UNIVERSITY
OF BRISTOL
LIBRARY

WITHDRAWN
24 JAN 2022
UNIVERSITY OF BRISTOL